OPTIMAL PROTECTION OF INTERNATIONAL LAW

Assume, for a moment, that the necessary tools are available to induce or even force states to comply with international law. In such a state of affairs, how strongly should international law be protected? More specifically, how easy should it be to change international law? Should treaties be specifically performed or should states be given an opportunity to "pay their way out"? In the event of states violating their commitments, what kind of back-up enforcement or sanctions should be imposed?

Joost Pauwelyn uses the distinction between liability rules, property protection and inalienable entitlements as a starting point for a new theory of variable protection of international law, placed at the intersection between "European absolutism" and "American voluntarism." Rather than undermining international law, variable protection takes the normativity of international law seriously and calibrates it to achieve maximum welfare and effectiveness at the lowest cost to contractual freedom and legitimacy.

JOOST PAUWELYN is Professor of International Law at the Graduate Institute of International and Development Studies, Geneva. Previously, he was a law professor at Duke University in the USA (2002–7) and an official with the World Trade Organization (1996–2002). In 2005, he received the Paul Guggenheim Prize for his book *Conflict of Norms in Public International Law* (2003).

OPTIMAL PROTECTION OF INTERNATIONAL LAW: NAVIGATING BETWEEN EUROPEAN ABSOLUTISM AND AMERICAN VOLUNTARISM

JOOST PAUWELYN

CAMBRIDGE
UNIVERSITY PRESS

CAMBRIDGE UNIVERSITY PRESS
Cambridge, New York, Melbourne, Madrid, Cape Town, Singapore, São Paulo, Delhi

Cambridge University Press
The Edinburgh Building, Cambridge CB2 8RU, UK

Published in the United States of America by Cambridge University Press, New York

www.cambridge.org
Information on this title: www.cambridge.org/9780521516822

First published 2008

Printed in the United Kingdom at the University Press, Cambridge

A catalogue record for this publication is available from the British Library

Library of Congress Cataloguing in Publication Data
Pauwelyn, Joost.
Optimal protection of international law: navigating between European absolutism and American voluntarism / Joost Pauwelyn.
p. cm.
Includes bibliographical references and index.
ISBN 978-0-521-51682-2 (hardback)
1. International law. I. Title.
KZ3410.P39 2008
341–dc22 2008028113

ISBN 978-0-521-51682-2 hardback

CONTENTS

TABLE OF CASES

Arbitration

European Court of First Instance

European Court of Justice

International Court of Justice

Advisory Proceedings

Contentious cases

Permanent Court of International Justice

United States

World Trade Organization

US – Gasoline

TABLE OF TREATIES

ACKNOWLEDGMENTS

This book in many ways reflects a personal itinerary in law and legal education. What I refer to in the book as European absolutism is very much the atmosphere in which I gained my legal education. European idealism also colored my early thinking about international law. My work as an international civil servant and, especially, the five years I spent in the United States as a professor of law opened the doors of what I call American voluntarism. And in some of my work, I eagerly explored American realism. The core objective of this book is to present a middle way between these two extremes by providing a more sophisticated way of thinking about the "binding nature" of international law. In essence, the book pleads for a variable scale of different levels and degrees of protection and enforcement of international law.

I would like to thank Daniel Bodansky, Howard Chang, Jeffrey Dunoff, Ralf Michaels, Eric Posner, Cesare Romano, Simon Schropp, Paul Stephan, Alec Stone Sweet, Joel Trachtman, Anne Van Aaken, Carlos Vazquez and the participants of workshops held at Tübingen University (Germany), the Max Planck Institute for Research on Collective Goods (Bonn), Chicago Law School, Duke Law, Georgetown Law Center, Georgia Law, Temple Law School and Yale Law School for their comments on an earlier version of this book. Deborah Upchurch and Luiz Salles have been extremely helpful in the editorial process. Obviously, all mistakes remain mine alone.

ABBREVIATIONS

AJIL	*American Journal of International Law*
Alabama LR	*Alabama Law Review*
Am Econ R	*American Economic Review*
Am L Econ R	*American Law and Economics Review*
Am Polit Sc R	*American Political Science Review*
Am Soc R	*American Sociological Review*
Arizona St LJ	*Arizona State Law Journal*
Austrian R Int Eur L	*Austrian Review of International and European Law*
BITs	Bilateral Investment Treaties
BYBIL	*British Yearbook of International Law*
California LR	*California Law Review*
Cardozo LR	*Cardozo Law Review*
CDM	Clean Development Mechanism
Chicago LR	*Chicago Law Review*
Columbia LR	*Columbia Law Review*
Cornell LR	*Cornell Law Review*
Denver J Int L Pol	*Denver Journal of International Law and Policy*
DRC	Democratic Republic of the Congo
DSR	Dispute Settlement Reports
DSU	Understanding on Rules and Procedures Governing the Settlement of Disputes
Duke LJ	*Duke Law Journal*
EC	European Communities
Econ Polit	*Economics and Politics*

EJIL	*European Journal of International Law*
ETS	European Treaty Series
European J Int L	*European Journal of International Law*
FAFT	Financial Action Task Force
Georgia J Int Comp L	*Georgia Journal of International and Comparative Law*
GAO	General Accounting Office
GAOR	General Assembly Official Records
GATS	General Agreement on Trade in Services
GATT	General Agreement on Tariffs and Trade
Georgetown Immigr LJ	*Georgetown Immigration Law Journal*
Harvard Hum Rts J	*Harvard Human Rights Journal*
Harvard Int LJ	*Harvard International Law Journal*
Harvard LR	*Harvard Law Review*
Hofstra LR	*Hofstra Law Review*
ICJ	International Court of Justice
ICJ Rep	ICJ Reports
ICSID	International Centre for the Settlement of Investment Disputes
ILC	International Law Commission
ILC Articles	ILC Articles on the Responsibility of States for Internationally Wrongful Acts
ILM	International Legal Materials
Int Rev L Econ	*International Review of Law and Economics*

IO	*International Organization*
JIEL	*Journal of International Economic Law*
JL Econ	*Journal of Law and Economics*
JL Econ Org	*Journal of Law and Economics Organization*
J Leg Stud	*Journal of Legal Studies*
J Polit Econ	*Journal of Political Economy*
J World Investment Trade	*Journal of World Investment and Trade*
L Econ Civ L Countries	*Law and Economics in Civil Law Countries*
Michigan LR	*Michigan Law Review*
Minnesota J Global Trade	*Minnesota Journal of Global Trade*
Minnesota LR	*Minnesota Law Review*
MIT Press	Massachusetts Institute of Technology Press
NAFTA	North American Free Trade Agreement
Nat Res J	*Natural Resources Journal*
Nordic J Int L	*Nordic Journal of International Law*
NY Times	*New York Times*
NYUJ Int L Polit	*New York University Journal of International Law and Politics*
NYULR	*New York University Law Review*
PCIJ Series	Permanent Court of International Justice Publication Series
Pub Pol	*Public Policy*
QJ Econ	*Quarterly Journal of Economics*

Recueil des Cours	*Recueil des Cours de l'académie de droit international*
SG Agreement	Agreement on Safeguards
SSRN	Social Science Research Network
Stanford LR	*Stanford Law Review*
Southern California LR	*Southern California Law Review*
Subsidies Agreement	Agreement on Subsidies and Countervailing Measures
Trans L Contemp Probs	*Transnational Law and Contemporary Problems*
TRIPS Agreement	Agreement on Trade-Related Aspects of Intellectual Property Rights
U Chicago LR	*University of Chicago Law Review*
UN	United Nations
UNCLOS	United Nations Convention on the Law of the Sea
UNESCO	United Nations Educational, Scientific and Cultural Organization
UNRIAA	United Nations Reports of International Arbitral Awards
UNTS	United Nations Treaty Series
U Pittsburgh LR	*University of Pittsburgh Law Review*
US	United States of America
USTR	United States Trade Representative
U St Thomas	University of Saint Thomas
Vanderbilt J Int L	*Vanderbilt Journal of International Law*
Vanderbilt LR	*Vanderbilt Law Review*

VCLT	Vienna Convention on the Law of Treaties
Virginia LR	*Virginia Law Review*
Wisconsin LR	*Wisconsin Law Review*
World Comp L Econ R	*World Competition Law and Economics Review*
WTO	World Trade Organization
Yale J Int L	*Yale Journal of International Law*
Yale LJ	*Yale Law Journal*
YB Int Env L	*Yearbook of International Environmental Law*
ZaöRV	*Zeitschrift für ausländisches öffentliches Recht und Völkerrecht*

FOREWORD

Should we allow for "efficient breach" in international law? That is one of the questions that Professor Joost Pauwelyn poses in *Optimal Protection of International Law.* If this question were asked by anyone named Posner, either Richard or Eric, or any of their fellow travelers, European international lawyers would shake their heads at American frivolity and even folly. They would wonder why so many Americans continue playing around with economic models of rules and contracts when the fragile edifice of international rules safeguarding the peace, health and welfare of the planet needs all the strengthening it can get. From their point of view, the optimal level of protection is clearly the strongest level of protection. American partisans of law and economics, on the other hand, would assume that the optimal level of protection is the level that allows for the greatest freedom of action. The actual knowledge or thinking of neither side would be advanced.

But Professor Pauwelyn is not an American international lawyer, or at least not of the traditional kind. He has taught at a leading American law school, but he is Belgian by birth, educated in Belgium, England and Switzerland, and a veteran of the legal affairs division of the World Trade Organization. He is thus deeply familiar with European approaches to international law and writes with a keen awareness of the standard transatlantic dichotomy between legal formalists and legal realists. Indeed, he constructs the ideal types of European absolutism, according to which rights under international law are inalienable and thus cannot be legally transferred or breached, and American voluntarism, which views all international legal rights as violable as long as the violator can be held liable and required to pay compensation. Pauwelyn chooses a middle path, steering his argument deftly between the two schools.

Therein lies part of the value of his work. He starts from the premise that international law is far stronger than European international lawyers are often prepared to recognize, strong enough to be able to support a more flexible enforcement structure that will allow the users of international law to meet their needs more effectively in a fast-changing international economic and political environment. But he also recognizes that not all international law, like not all domestic law, should be up for grabs, violable at will according to the dictates of an individual agent's cost-benefit analysis.

Pauwelyn wants to move beyond the question of whether international law is law or legally binding, preferring instead to examine issues of allocation, protection, and back-up enforcement. He asks:

1 How does international law allocate entitlements?
2 How does international law protect entitlements?
3 What happens if international rules of protection are disregarded?

The simplicity and clarity of this model cuts refreshingly through the thicket of state responsibility, and leads him to a surprising result. He concludes: "The simple rule is that, as in domestic law, by default, entitlements under international law ought to be protected by a property rule" – a rule that no one can take or infringe an entitlement without the consent of the rights holder. This default rule "is justified by principles of contractual freedom, welfare maximization and the fact that property protection requires the least amount of intervention."

Many readers may assume at this point that Pauwelyn is an international minimalist, aimed at loosing the fragile bonds that hold the international order together. The standard assumption – typically unstated but still strongly held – is that law and economics types don't really want law at all; or at least no more than the bare minimum necessary for a market to function. Yet one of the most important contributions of *Optimal Protection of International Law* is Pauwelyn's exploration of the paradox of why the strongest international law rules may have the weakest enforcement regimes. *Jus cogens* rules, the holy of holies binding the entire international community, are protected as inalienable rights of all peoples and the community obligation of all nations. Yet when *jus cogens* is violated, the only responses available are reparations and proportional countermeasures. If one nation commits crimes against humanity, however, other nations cannot commit crimes against humanity in retaliation. And although in theory any nation can demand reparations from a nation violating its obligations to the entire community, in practice any one nation can look to its neighbors to blow the whistle, creating a collective action problem.

The paradoxical result is that elevating a rule or norm to the status of *jus cogens* may actually result in reducing the protection afforded by the rule and weakening its enforcement. Pauwelyn thus argues that supporters of stronger enforcement for the kinds of rules that are currently *jus cogens* – against slavery, genocide, crimes against humanity – should consider maintaining a property regime. This is just one example of the importance of examining each international legal rule or cluster of rules on its own terms, carefully assessing the enforcement options available and the proper alignment of incentives. In Pauwelyn's words, "international law has reached a degree of maturity that gives it the luxury, indeed, the obligation, of variable protection."

In short, we have a European international lawyer taking a highly nuanced approach to the enforcement of international law (that in itself is not so unusual – Pauwelyn himself recognizes that his label of "European absolutists" is something of a caricature) based on largely American law and economics theory. He develops strong arguments for expanding a property rights approach as an indicator of the health and growing strength of international law. This is a set of positions that defies easy categorization, a mark of strong scholarship.

Looking forward, the readiest application of Pauwelyn's analysis is in regime design, an area of international law and international relations scholarship that is attracting increasing attention in the US. Indeed, the leader to turn first to regime theory and later to institutionalism more generally, Robert Keohane, gave the Castle Lectures at Yale Law School in the fall of 2007 on Institutional Design and Power. Pauwelyn provides a matrix that will be pure gold for scholars and practitioners seeking to diagnose particular types of international problems and sketch the basic architecture (or set of reforms to existing architecture) of institutions to resolve them.

Beyond these specific uses of the book, I suspect that scholars twenty years from now will look back and see *Optimal Protection of International Law* as part of a larger watershed: the convergence of European and American approaches to international law and international relations, based on a willingness to borrow from theoretical schools in multiple disciplines. Pauwelyn is young, energetic and productive. His work promises an era in which international lawyers from many different countries can draw on multiple literatures to formulate rules governing different areas of international life and design systems aimed at encouraging maximum compliance with minimal enforcement. Their work will transcend the debates between traditional jurisprudence and law and economics, and between partisans of different schools of international relations theory – rationalism versus constructivism, realism versus institutionalism and liberalism.

In closing, it is worth reflecting on the questions Pauwelyn does not ask. He does not bother with the meta-questions of whether international law is really law, or whether it can be disentangled from international politics. He does not interrogate the nature of sovereignty or the nature of power. He instead takes as his starting point the existence of a set of legal rules that confer entitlements and regulate behavior in the international arena – rules that he has seen operate at first hand in his professional life. He shows how they differ from but also how they resemble domestic law and explores the reasons behind both the differences and the similarities. And he assumes that international law, like domestic law, can benefit from the insights of economics, politics, sociology, and game theory.

Finally, instead of asking why Americans and Europeans diverge so from one another, he builds a bridge between them. Bravo!

Anne-Marie Slaughter
Dean
Woodrow Wilson School of Public
and International Affairs
Princeton University
Shanghai, March 2008

Introduction

International law scholarship has long been obsessed with trying to explain and predict *why* and *when* states comply with international law.[1] Is it because of pure self-interest,[2] reputation,[3] or domestic pressure groups and internalization,[4] or perhaps explained by a sense of legal obligation or the legitimacy of the norm itself,[5] or rather due to

1 For a review of the literature on compliance, see Kal Raustiala and Anne-Marie Slaughter, "International Law, International Relations and Compliance," in Walter Carlsnaes *et al.* (eds.), *Handbook of International Relations* (London: Sage, 2002), 538; Abram Chayes and Antonia Handler Chayes, *The New Sovereignty: Compliance with International Regulatory Agreements* (Cambridge, Mass.: Harvard University Press, 1995); Michael Zurn and Christian Joerges (eds.), *Law and Governance in Postnational Europe: Compliance beyond the Nation-State* (Cambridge: Cambridge University Press, 2005); Oona Hathawa, "Do Human Rights Treaties Make a Difference?" (2002) 111 *Yale LJ* 1935; Ryan Goodman and Derek Jinks, "How To Influence States: Socialization and International Human Rights Law" (2004) 54 *Duke LJ* 621.

2 Jack Goldsmith and Eric Posner, *The Limits of International Law* (Oxford: Oxford University Press, 2005).

3 Andrew Guzman, "International Law: A Compliance Based Theory" (2002), 90 *California LR* 1,823.

4 Harold Koh, "Why Do Nations Obey International Law?" (1997), 106 *Yale LJ* 2,599; Beth Simmons, "International Law and State Behavior: Commitment and Compliance in International Monetary Affairs" (2000), 94 *Am Polit Sc R* 819; Claire R. Kelly, "Enmeshment as a Theory of Compliance" (2005), 37 *NYUJ Int L Polit* 303.

5 Thomas Franck, *The Power of Legitimacy among Nations* (New York: Oxford University Press, 1990).

bureaucratic networks[6] or the personal psychology of political leaders?[7] This approach has consistently overlooked a logically preceding but no less important question: assuming, for a moment, that the necessary tools are available to induce or even force states to comply – whatever these tools may be, based on one's theory of compliance – how strongly *should* international law be protected? In other words, how strongly *should* states bind themselves to international law? I deliberately use the broader terms "protect" and "bind" as I want them to cover three distinct questions:

1 How easy should it be to create and change international law?
2 Must international law always be specifically performed or should states be given an opportunity to "pay their way out"?
3 In the event states do violate their commitments, what kind of back-up enforcement or sanctions should be imposed?

In recent decades, international law has come to address the full panoply of concerns of the regulatory state, ranging from individual human rights to the domestic regulation of commerce and the environment.[8] Faced with similar expansion and diversity, no single domestic legal

[6] Anne-Marie Slaughter, *A New World Order* (Princeton: Princeton University Press, 2004); Manuel Castells, *The Rise of the Network Society* (Oxford: Blackwell, 1996).

[7] William Bradford, "In the Minds of Men: A Theory of Compliance with the Laws of War" (2004), 36 *Arizona St LJ* 1,243, at 1,438 ("much of the variation in compliance is attributable to personality" of government leaders).

[8] See Joseph Weiler, "The Geology of International Law – Governance, Democracy and Legitimacy" (2004), 64 *ZaöRV* 547.

system requires absolute protection, or imposes the same sanctions, for all legal commitments. Constitutions are normally written in stone, while contracts can simply be renegotiated. Where certain statutory obligations can be bought off, others, such as those under criminal law, cannot be transferred as between private individuals. Theft is sanctioned more heavily than breach of contract, and remedies for constitutional violation are more forceful than those for statutory breach. Considering the current state of international law, in contrast, the levels and types of protection or "bindingness" of international law commitments are surprisingly uniform (besides so-called soft law, a set of norms not tackled in this book). Yet, in recent decades, some variations have emerged. The aim of this book is to elaborate a framework of variable protection for international law based on current examples as well as analogies with legal scholarship centered on domestic legal systems. Far from a concession to weakness, variable protection of international law is the logical result of its success and further refinement. Rather than undermining international law, variable protection takes the normativity of international law seriously and calibrates it to achieve maximum welfare and effectiveness at the lowest cost to contractual freedom and legitimacy.[9]

One of the truly attractive features of international law is that, with the drafting of each new treaty, negotiators

[9] As Ernest Young notes: "The point is to take international law seriously as law, by subjecting it to the same sorts of institutional give and take that have characterized our domestic legal arrangements throughout our history" (Ernest Young, "Institutional Settlement in a Globalizing Judicial System" (2005), 54 *Duke LJ* 1,143, at 1,259).

are largely free to design their own type and level of protection as well as corresponding monitoring and/or sanctions regimes to back-up enforcement. It is with this flexibility in mind that one can realistically hope that the framework and proposals in this book can actually be implemented, one treaty at a time.

1

Overview and relevance of the analysis

In domestic law, the central question that this book seeks to answer – how strongly should international law be protected and enforced? – was addressed in the early 1970s in a seminal *Harvard Law Review* article by Guido Calabresi and Douglas Melamed.[1] Much like Hohfeld sixty years before them,[2] Calabresi and Melamed warned against indiscriminate use of the term legal "right." Yet, whereas Hohfeld distinguished between rights (corresponding to a duty), privileges, powers and immunities, Calabresi and Melamed referred to a broad pool of legal "entitlements." In their view, all of law can be seen as rules for the ownership and exchange (forcible or voluntary) of entitlements. They used the term "entitlements" instead of "rights" as the very purpose of their analysis was to discern different types of legal rights based on the degree of legal protection that they enjoy. As the common usage of the term "right" often corresponds to just one type of entitlement (namely those protected by a so-called property rule), the broader term of entitlements was needed

[1] Guido Calabresi and A. Douglas Melamed, "Property Rules, Liability Rules, and Inalienability: One View of the Cathedral" (1972), 85 *Harvard LR* 1,089.

[2] See Wesley N. Hohfeld, "Some Fundamental Legal Conceptions as Applied in Judicial Reasoning" (1913), 23 *Yale LJ 16*, and 26 *Yale LJ* (1917) 710.

to avoid confusion and to encapsulate not just one but all types of entitlements.[3]

Calabresi and Melamed provided a three-step scale of protection for domestic legal entitlements. In their view, a first group of entitlements is best protected as "inalienable," that is, not to be changed or transferred at all, not even if the entitlement's holder agrees. A second group is best protected as "property" or under a property rule, that is, it can be changed or taken, but only with the consent of the entitlement's holder. Optimal protection of a third group of entitlements is a so-called "liability rule," that is, the entitlement can be taken by anyone subject only to the obligation to pay full compensation for it.

The idea of protecting entitlements under a mere liability rule, pursuant to a take-and-pay principle, is reflected in the broader theory of "efficient breach." This theory, derived from the broader law and economics approach, holds that when the net cost of compliance is higher than the net cost of breach, breach must be tolerated, even promoted, as it serves the social function of maximizing overall welfare. If, in this scenario, the victim of breach is fully compensated, breach is, moreover, said to be Pareto desirable: while the violating

[3] More specifically, using the term "entitlements" enables the introduction of liability rules, as under a liability rule (say, a pollution tax) I do not have a legal "right" to clean air (which corresponds to a duty not to pollute), only a legal "entitlement" to clean air which anyone can take away for as long as compensation (i.e., the pollution tax) is paid. Thus, my legal entitlement to clean air does not correspond to a duty not to pollute; but rather to a duty to pay a tax in case one pollutes. Put differently, rather than a duty not to pollute, companies then have a right to pollute for as long as they pay the pollution tax.

party increases its welfare, the victim is made whole. In other words, the taker of the entitlement values it more than its current holder; hence, even after compensating the holder, the taker – and with it overall welfare – is still better off. Therefore, transfer is socially desirable and must be promoted even without the consent of the current entitlement holder. To have a property right, in contrast, is to have an entitlement that is in some important way shielded from such felicific or wealth-maximizing social functions.[4] Ronald Dworkin captured the vital importance of property rule protection when he coined the phrase "rights trump utility."[5] In other words, the idea of protecting entitlements as property (you cannot just take my car and leave behind the money for me to buy a new one, even if you think you value my car more than I do) corresponds to the market-based idea that property, individual rights and contractual freedom – not state intervention – are the best way to increase overall welfare. Property protection is, if you wish, the world of free trade, Adam Smith's invisible hand, a reflection of liberal capitalism. Protecting entitlements as inalienable or under a liability rule, in contrast, corresponds to market intervention by the state or some higher authority either by preventing entitlement holders to sell their entitlement (inalienability) or by letting the state or other people take or expropriate entitlements subject only to compensation in

[4] Michael Krauss, "Property Rules vs. Liability Rules," in B. Bouckaert and G. De Geest (eds.), *Encyclopedia of Law and Economics* (Cheltenham: Edward Elgar, 1999).

[5] Ronald Dworkin, *Taking Rights Seriously* (Cambridge, Mass.: Harvard University Press, 1975).

pursuit of overall welfare (liability rule). Whereas property protection reflects liberal capitalism, both inalienability and liability protection reflect social interventionism.[6]

The objective of this book is to apply the Calabresi and Melamed analysis, including the theory of efficient breach and the contrasting approaches of market-based exchange versus collective intervention, not to entitlements derived from *domestic* law but to entitlements accorded under *international* law. In other words, if a treaty allocates an "entitlement"[7] to free trade, to non-discrimination or to be free from certain environmental harm or human rights abuse, what is the best way to protect this entitlement? Should it be made "inalienable" or protected only as "property" or, rather, should it benefit from the weaker form of "liability" protection? In addition, if the cost of compliance outweighs the cost of breach – including the cost of fully compensating all victims – should a country be permitted to violate international law on the ground that breach is then efficient, even Pareto desirable? Is international law founded on market-based exchanges of entitlements (property rules) or does it, or should it, also include collective interventions that transcend

[6] For an indication that inalienability goes against traditional capitalism, see one of Ronald Reagan's favorite lines in election speeches: "Government exists to protect us from each other. Where government has gone beyond its limits is in deciding to protect us from ourselves": quoted in Alan Greenspan, *The Age of Turbulence* (New York: Penguin, 2007), at 87. Protecting "us from ourselves" is exactly what happens under inalienability, namely: even the entitlement holder herself cannot agree to transfer the entitlement.

[7] See *supra* note 3 on the distinction between entitlements and rights.

state-to-state bargaining and consent, in pursuit of overall welfare (liability rules) or so as to protect states from themselves (inalienability)? Do these models, which originate in domestic law, find application in international law? Must they be adapted or do they even become completely inappropriate? Descriptively, how does international law currently protect entitlements? Does this current level of protection accord to the predictions under the Calabresi and Melamed model? Does it conform to the theory of efficient breach?

These are the questions addressed in this book. They worry as much about *over*-protection of international law as about *under*-protection of international law. For a system long plagued by claims of irrelevance, such inquiry has understandably been somewhat of a taboo. Why worry about optimal protection, let alone over-protection, if international law is generally perceived as weak? Why nitpick over remedies if, in most cases, there is no compulsory dispute settlement system to establish breach in the first place? In recent years, however, the conventional wisdom that international law is weak has been seriously contested. The creation in 1994 of the World Trade Organization (WTO) and its compulsory dispute settlement system is often referred to as a major advance in the legalization of international affairs.[8] In a recent book,

[8] John Jackson, *The World Trading System: Law and Policy of International Economic Relations*, 2nd edn (Cambridge, Mass.: MIT Press, 1997), at 110; Judith Goldstein *et al.*, "Introduction: Legalization and World Politics" (2001), 54 *IO* 385, at 389 (referring to a victory for trade "legalists" over trade "pragmatists"). For a discussion on the evolution of law and politics in the world trading system: Joost Pauwelyn, "The Transformation of World Trade" (2005), 104 *Michigan LR* 1.

Professors Robert Scott and Paul Stephan, referring to the establishment of international criminal tribunals, investment and intellectual property rights protection with compulsory arbitration, European economic and human rights integration, and domestic civil litigation involving international law, go as far as concluding that

> [i]nternational law has become hard law, with its own Leviathan . . . The trend is clearly away from impotence. International law, because of the growth of formal enforcement, has become a real force with direct and material consequences for a wide range of actors.[9]

International law can, therefore, increasingly afford the luxury of asking itself: how strongly *should* entitlements be protected?[10] Harder international law is not necessarily better international law. In the Kyoto Protocol, for example, reductions in harmful emissions were not protected by an outright prohibition to

[9] Robert Scott and Paul Stephan, *The Limits of Leviathan* (Cambridge: Cambridge University Press, 2006), at 11 and 14. Scott and Stephan define "formal enforcement" as enforcement with private standing and a tribunal empowered to impose direct sanctions (at 367).

[10] See, in support, Andrew Guzman, "The Design of International Agreements" (2005), 16 *EJIL* 612; and Kal Raustiala, "Form and Substance in International Agreements" (2005), 99 *AJIL* 541. Even if one holds the view (further contested below in chapter 6) that international law continues to be weak – for example, because it lacks central enforcement – so that finer distinctions in normativity are irrelevant, the questions addressed in this book at least raise an interesting thought experiment. Imagine, for a moment, that you do have all necessary instruments in hand to force states to comply with their international commitments (whatever these instruments may be): how far would you go, and what criteria would guide you?

emit beyond a certain ceiling ("command-and-control," with elements of inalienability protection). Rather, the treaty imposed a certain ceiling for each country but then introduced the hotly debated notion of tradable emission rights allowing countries to pollute, even above their ceiling, for as long as they "pay" for it by means of emission credits ("cap-and-trade," grounded in the market-based idea of property rights and with some elements of liability protection).[11] Equally, in the WTO a fierce debate is raging as to whether the treaty requires countries to bring their trade policies in line with WTO disciplines (specific performance under a property rule) or whether it permits, or even promotes, countries to "buy-off" their WTO obligations by paying compensation or suffering equivalent trade retaliation (efficient breach under a liability rule).[12] Even

[11] The system of tradable allowances was originally proposed by the United States and objected to by many, especially in Europe. See Jonathan Wiener, "Global Environmental Regulation: Instrument Choice in Legal Context" (1999), 108 *Yale LJ* 677, at 712 and references in note 144. For a critique see Michael J. Sandel, Editorial, "It's Immoral To Buy the Right To Pollute," *NY Times*, 15 December 1997, at A23; and "Sins of Emission," *The Economist*, 5–11 August 2006, at 15 ("critics of offsetting argue that the ability to buy retrospective forgiveness for sins of emission is no substitute for not sinning in the first place").

[12] Contrast, in particular, Warren Schwartz and Alan Sykes, "The Economic Structure of Renegotiation and Dispute Resolution in the World Trade Organization" (2002), 31 *J Leg Stud* 179 (arguing that the WTO is a liability rule system that promotes efficient breach) to John Jackson, "International Law Status of WTO Dispute Settlement Reports: Obligation To Comply or Option To 'Buy Out'?" (2004), 98 *AJIL* 109 (arguing that the WTO imposes a property rule with an obligation to perform). Uncertainty as to the goal of WTO dispute settlement has, in turn, led to case law on the level of permitted trade

in the field of international refugee law, the idea of tradable quotas was floated. To share the burden of refugees more equitably amongst potential host countries, Peter Schuck has, for example, suggested allocating country-specific refugee quotas, and creating a market where states who are unwilling or unable to host their share of refugees can purchase credits from other states who do want to accept more refugees.[13] Similarly, the FAO Treaty on Plant Genetic Resources for Food and Agriculture currently protects the use of sixty-four major crops and forages and their genetic diversity not by handing out exclusive property rights but through a liability rule regime that provides open access to the covered plant resources subject to payment or benefit-sharing when, for example, a patented commercial product is developed using these resources.[14]

sanctions in response to WTO breach that is in a state of disarray. One recent arbitration panel openly admitted this confusion as follows: "it is not completely clear what role is to be played by the suspension of obligations in the DSU and a large part of the conceptual debate that took place in these proceedings could have been avoided if a clear 'object and purpose' were identified" (*US – Byrd Amendment*, Arbitration under DSU Article 22.6, para. 6.4).

[13] Peter H. Schuck, "Refugee Burden-Sharing: A Modest Proposal" (1997), 22 *Yale J Int L* 243, at 270–1. For a critique, see Benjamin Cook, "Methods in Its Madness: The Endowment Effect in an Analysis of Refugee Burden-Sharing and Proposed Refugee Market" (2004), 19 *Georgetown Immigr LJ* 333; and for a response to criticism, see Peter H. Schuck, "A Response to the Critics" (1999), 12 *Harvard Hum Rts J* 385.

[14] See the International Treaty on Plant Genetic Resources for Food and Agriculture, adopted 3 November 2001, entry into force 29 June 2004, FAO/RES/3 (2001), available at www.fao.org/AG/cgrfa/itpgr.htm (last visited 28 December 2007).

Let it also be clear what this book is *not* about. Although I will be using the two extremes of what I call European absolutism (international entitlements should be inalienable) and American voluntarism (international entitlements are, at best, protected by a mere liability rule), this book is not about the age-old question of whether international law is "law" or whether rules of international law are "legally binding." When negotiators design treaties and set the way in which entitlements are to be protected (inalienability, property rule or liability rule), they define and specify the scope, content and reach of the rights and obligations that derive from the treaty. Protecting an entitlement under a liability rule does not make the treaty provision less important or less "law"; it only defines how and how strongly the entitlement will be protected.[15] As a result, to permit the taking of an entitlement under a liability rule (e.g., pollution under a pollution tax) is not the same as tolerating breach of a treaty obligation. Rather, the taking of the entitlement (in our case, pollution) remains within the terms of the original contract (it is *intra*-contractual and perfectly legal); breach is only committed (i.e., *extra*-contractual behavior only occurs) in case the taker does not pay compensation for the entitlement (e.g., in case the polluter does not pay the tax). Conversely, the classification of an entitlement as inalienable does not make the rule in question more important or more "law"; it only

[15] In this sense, liability protection has nothing to do with so-called soft law. Soft law, generally understood, does not meet the threshold of a legally binding norm. In contrast, an entitlement protected by a liability rule constitutes a legally binding norm; the distinguishing feature of the entitlement is rather the *degree* of legal protection that it enjoys.

prevents states from transferring the entitlement on a bilateral basis, that is, from altering or contracting out of the rule in question *inter se*. Finally, in case an entitlement is protected by a property rule, to transfer the entitlement by mutual consent (i.e., to amend a treaty or modify it *inter se*) is not the same as breaching the treaty. In this case, breach occurs only when the entitlement is taken *without* consent. Efficient breach, on the other hand, at least if we take the term at face value, does describe a particular type of *violation* of the law, namely one that increases welfare without making anyone worse off. The theory of efficient breach thereby questions the legally binding nature of the law. Yet, where a legal system permits or even promotes efficient breach (that is, it imposes a liability rule), by definition, "efficient breach" no longer constitutes an extra-contractual violation of the rules; rather, what would otherwise be considered as breach then becomes a simple taking of an entitlement *with* full compensation as required under liability protection. In that sense, the term "breach" in "efficient breach" in those cases where entitlements are protected by a liability rule is a misnomer: there is no breach; only intra-contractual behavior that triggers an obligation to compensate, and only if no such compensation is made can we speak of breach or extra-contractual behavior.

Chapter 2 of this book defines the two extremes of what I call European absolutism and American voluntarism. Chapter 3 explains the Calabresi and Melamed framework and redefines and expands it for application in international law. Within this framework, chapter 4 asks the normative question of how international law entitlements ought to be protected. Chapter 5 tests these normative predictions against the current state of protection of international law. Chapter 6 assesses the rules of back-up enforcement of international law, that is, how international law reacts to extra-contractual behavior, that is, in case the rules of protection are flouted. Chapter 7 concludes and summarizes the main findings of this book.

2

The two extremes of European absolutism and American voluntarism

Ask anyone how strongly international law ought to be protected, and the chances are that you get one of two answers. Both would likely start with, "what kind of a question is this?" A first standard answer would explain that international law remains weak, that we do not see enough compliance anyhow, and that more compliance or harder law is by definition better; indeed, merely posing the question of how strongly international law should be protected risks undermining the binding nature of international law itself. A second group of people would find the question equally disturbing as, from their perspective, international law is not even law, given that it lacks central enforcement; thus, any discussion of variable levels of protection is a waste of time, as states will anyhow violate international law whenever they want to.

The first school of thought, driven to its extreme, is what I will call European absolutism. This is an extreme version of the constitutional approach to international law which holds that, once allocated, international entitlements cannot be modified or traded. Rather, they must be specifically performed unless, in the case of treaties, all treaty parties agree to reallocate the entitlement. Put differently, on this view, all international entitlements should, to some degree, be inalienable. Hugo Grotius, for example, one of the (European) founders of international law, largely equated the new discipline with natural law and noted that, in his view, this "law of nature ... is unchangeable, even in the sense that it cannot be changed by God."[1]

The second school of thought, driven to its own extreme, I will refer to as American voluntarism. This is an extreme version of the contractual approach to international law, according to which the allocation of international entitlements is a mere pledge which states can renege on, based on a simple cost-benefit analysis.[2] On this view, international entitlements are, at best, protected by a simple liability rule, a contract that can be broken with the payment of compensation.[3]

[1] H. Grotius, *De Jure Belli ac Pacis, Libri Tres*, book 1, ch. 1, X.5 ("[e]st autem jus naturale adeo immutabile, ut ne a deo quidem mutari queat").

[2] See, for example, Hans Morgenthau, *Politics among Nations: The Struggle for Power and Peace* (New York: A. A. Knopf, 1948), and John Mearsheimer, *The Tragedy of Great Power Politics* (New York: W. W. Norton, 2001), representing the so-called realist school which regards legal constraints beyond the nation-state as non-existent or at best very weak. As John Bolton, at the time of writing US ambassador to the UN, put it more bluntly: "International law is not law; it is a series of political and moral arrangements that stand or fall on their own merits, and anything else is simply theology and superstition masquerading as law" (John Bolton, "Is There Really 'Law' in International Affairs?" (2000), 10 *Trans L Contemp Probs* 1, at 48).

[3] Joel P. Trachtman, "Building the WTO Cathedral" (2006), available at SSRN: http://ssrn.com/abstract=815844, at p. 21 (discussing remedies in general international law and concluding that "the goal seems to be to induce compliance when compliance is efficient, and breach when it is not"); and Warren Schwartz and Alan Sykes, "The Economic Structure of Renegotiation and Dispute Resolution in the World Trade Organization" (2002), 31 *J Leg Stud* 179, at 192 ("the WTO system contemplates departures from specified obligations when the costs of compliance exceed the associated benefits").

I fully realize that, today, few informed observers of international law fall in either of these two extremes. I only offer these extremes as signposts or Weberian ideal-types within which I will situate and contrast my own propositions. Obviously, there are Europeans with voluntarist traits and Americans that have an absolutist bent,[4] as well as Europeans and Americans who fall somewhere in between.[5] Yet, for ease of reference and, I admit, dramatic effect, my generalization identifies absolutism with Europe and voluntarism with the United States of America.[6]

[4] John Jackson (see, for example, "International Law Status of WTO Dispute Settlement Reports: Obligation To Comply or Option To 'Buy Out'?" (2004), 98 *AJIL* 109), tends more toward European absolutism than American voluntarism. Equally, Jacob Cogan, a US State Department official, starts his article ("Noncompliance and the International Rule of Law" (2006), 31 *Yale J Int L* 189) with the following: "We treat noncompliance with disdain, and for good reason. After all, what does it mean to be a law if violation is permitted? And what does it mean to be a legal system if disobedience is tolerated?").

[5] The present author, for example, has previously explored both European absolutism: see Joost Pauwelyn, "Enforcement and Countermeasures in the WTO: Rules Are Rules – Towards a More Collective Approach" (2000), 94 *AJIL* 621; and American voluntarism: see Joost Pauwelyn, "A Typology of Multilateral Treaty Obligations: Are WTO Obligations Bilateral or Collective in Nature?" (2003), 14 *EJIL* 907.

[6] For a representative sample on the differences between Europe and America in their approach to international law, see Robert Kagan, *Paradise and Power: America and Europe in the New World Order* (New York: A. A. Knopf, 2003); Jeremy Rifkin, *The European Dream: How Europe's Vision of the Future Is Quietly Eclipsing the American Dream* (New York: J. P. Tarcher/Penguin, 2004); Jed Rubenfeld, "Unilateralism and Constitutionalism" (2004), 79 *NYULR* 1,971; and Robert J. Delahunty, "The Battle of Mars and Venus: Why Do American and

The first extreme (absolutism) is closely aligned to traditional supporters of international law, haunted by the critique that "their" discipline has no teeth and is, therefore, largely irrelevant. In response, and somewhat paradoxically, this group portrays inalienability and specific performance as the ideal or optimal level of protection of international entitlements. In the same spirit, this camp pursues *harder* international law as necessarily *better* international law, and advocates the constitutionalization of international law as a source of supreme law that ties the hands of governments to protect themselves against political, economic and other forms of government failure.[7] Though crudely generalizing, I call this approach European absolutism, both because of how many European academics analyze and promote international law, and because of how the law of the European Communities (EC) has been constructed: although EC treaties can be amended, individual member states cannot contract out of EC treaties *inter se* and EC law has direct effect and supremacy in domestic legal orders. In addition, under civil law (prevalent in most European countries) the fall-back remedy for breach is, equally, specific performance, not compensation,[8] and

European Attitudes toward International Law Differ?" (2006), University of Saint Thomas Legal Studies Research Paper No. 06–15, available at http://ssrn.com/abstract=899404.

[7] See, for example, E.-U. Petersmann, *Constitutional Functions and Constitutional Problems of International Economic Law* (Fribourg: Imprim. St-Paul, 1991).

[8] G. H. Treitel, *Remedies for Breach of Contract: A Comparative Account* (Oxford: Clarendon, 1988), at 43–74, and noting, at p. 51, for example, that "German law starts with the principle that the creditor is entitled to a judgment for performance."

the renegotiation of contracts is generally discouraged.[9] Many developing countries have long sympathized with this approach, as they tend to regard international law as an instrument to level global political imbalances. From that vantage point as well, protecting international entitlements as inalienable has often been advocated.[10]

The second extreme (voluntarism) is closely aligned to traditional critics of international law who question the ability of international law to influence the conduct of states. For this group, international law is a patchwork of pledges or, at best, contracts, that ultimately have little or no impact on state behavior.[11] Given the absence of centralized enforcement and the requirements of state sovereignty and representative democracy, the argument goes, international entitlements cannot be – nor should they be – fully protected in all cases.[12]

[9] Eric Brousseau, "Did the Common Law biased [*sic*] the Economics of Contract . . . and May It Change?" (2001), 6 *L Econ Civ L Countries* 79, at 83–5.

[10] For a discussion, see Robert Hudec, *Developing Countries in the GATT Legal System* (Aldershot: Gower, 1987).

[11] See, for example, Jack Goldsmith and Eric Posner, *The Limits of International Law* (Oxford: Oxford University Press, 2005), at 3: "Put briefly, our theory is that international law emerges from states acting rationally to maximize their interests, given their perception of the interests of other states and the distribution of state power." And at p. 9 rejecting arguments that "the preferences of individuals, and therefore state interests, can be influenced by international law and institutions."

[12] Or as John Bolton put it: "claims that 'international law' has binding and authoritative force ultimately ring either hollow or unacceptable to a free people": John Bolton, "Is There Really 'Law' in International Affairs?" (2000), 10 *Trans L Contemp Probs* 1, at 9).

Based on a cost-benefit analysis, this camp predicts that states will only comply with international law if the costs of its defection outweigh those of compliance. Along the same lines, the normative position of many within this second school of thought is that a state *should, a fortiori*, only comply with international law if, overall, it makes its people better off.[13] Hence, on this view, when designing treaties or the system of international law more generally, states should be permitted, even advised, to take the entitlements of other states for as long as the compensation to be paid for such taking falls below the benefit derived from the taking.[14] Whilst European absolutists would regard such a take-and-pay principle as close to immoral,[15] for American voluntarists "efficient

[13] See, for example, Alan M. Dershowitz, *Why Terrorism Works* (New Haven: Yale University Press, 2002), arguing that the laws against torture should be subject to exception where the cost of compliance is too great. Equally, in the domestic law context, some have argued to extend liability rules so as to cover also constitutional rights. See Eugene Kontorovich, "The Constitution in Two Dimensions: A Transaction Cost Analysis of Constitutional Remedies" (2005), 91 *Virginia LR* 1,135.

[14] See *supra*, chapter 1 note 12. That efficient breach is more attractive to US, common law lawyers than it is to lawyers from the European, civil law tradition, see Aristides Hatzis, "Civil Law and Economic Reasoning: An Unlikely Pair," Working paper dated February 6, 2005, available at http://papers.ssrn.com/sol3/papers.cfm?abstract_id=661661.

[15] See, for example, Michael J. Sandel, Editorial, "It's Immoral To Buy the Right To Pollute," *NY Times*, 15 December 1997, at A23 and "Sins of Emission," *The Economist*, 5–11 August 2006, at 15 (noting that some environmentalists denounce the "offsetting" of carbon emissions under the Kyoto Protocol as comparable to "the sale of indulgences by the Catholic church in the early 16th century, whereby people could,

breach" improves overall welfare without making anyone worse off, and ought therefore not only to be permitted but to be actively promoted. From this perspective, full performance is therefore anything but optimal performance.

Though once again crudely generalizing, I call this approach American voluntarism because of the United States' skepticism toward international law and its self-proclaimed strategy of "coalitions of the willing."[16] It is also based on the supremacy of US law over international law (most treaties signed by the United States are not self-executing[17] and, in any event, US federal law prevails over earlier international law[18]) and the pervading law and economics approach in the US legal academy. In addition, in the common law (and in contrast to civil law), the fall-back remedy for breach is, equally,

in effect, purchase forgiveness of past sins by handing over enough money").

[16] See, for example, Guy Dinmore, "US Sees Coalitions of the Willing as Best Ally," *Financial Times*, 5 January 2006 (quoting a senior US State Department official as follows: "We 'ad hoc' our way through coalitions of the willing. That's the future").

[17] See, for example, Curtis Bradley, "*Breard*, Our Dualist Constitution, and the Internationalist Conception" (1999), 51 *Stanford LR* 529, at 531: "the U.S. approach to international law has been and continues to be fundamentally dualist"; at 540: "One condition frequently attached by U.S. treaty-makers is that the treaty in question not be self-executing . . . for example, U.S. treaty-makers have attached 'non-self-execution' declarations to their ratification of several human rights treaties"; and Andrea Bianchi, "International Law and U.S. Courts: The Myth of Lohengrin Revisited" (2004), 15 *EJIL* 751.

[18] The later-in-time rule is often traced to *Taylor v. Morton*, 23 F. Cas. 784 (C.C. Mass. 1855) (No. 13, 799), 67 US 481(1862).

expectation damages, not specific performance,[19] and the renegotiation of contracts is encouraged (parties cannot ban future modifications).[20]

Put another way, European absolutism strongly believes in law and pre-commitment and, in pursuit of Kantian ideals, wants to dissect international law as much as possible from politics. In this vein, it regards international law as reflecting universal values to which domestic legal systems, prone to majoritarian abuse (witness the democratically elected Hitler), must be tied as a higher law.[21] Hence, for this school of thought, international law ought, ideally, to be sacredly protected and specifically performed. American voluntarism, in contrast, strongly believes in politics and

[19] Treitel, *Remedies for Breach of Contract*, at 63: "In common law jurisdictions, the normal remedies for breach of contract are the action for an agreed sum . . . and the action for damages." See also Oliver Wendell Holmes, *The Common Law*, ed. Mark D. Howe ([1881] Cambridge, Mass.: Belknap Press, 1963), at 236: "The only universal consequence of a legally binding promise is that the law makes the promisor pay damages if the promised event does not come to pass."

[20] Alan Schwartz and Robert Scott, "Contract Theory and the Limits of Contract Law" (2003), 113 *Yale LJ* 541, at 611: parties are "not formally free to prevent themselves from modifying their contract in the future." See Restatement (Second) of Contracts and 311 cmt. a (1979).

[21] See, for example, Martin Shapiro and Alec Stone Sweet, *On Law, Politics, and Judicialization* (New York: Oxford University Press, 2002), at 203: "European academic lawyers labour continuously to separate law from politics and, by extension, to distinguish what constitutional courts do from what political institutions do."

flexibility and, in a more critical approach to law generally,[22] subjects even its highest law, that is, the US constitution, to politics, deliberation and consent. As a result, optimal protection of international law involves a constant cost-benefit analysis and is anything but full performance.

It is not the objective of this book to explain why Europe and the United States approach international law differently. Rubenfeld has recently described the divergence as grounded in profoundly different constitutional traditions.[23] In Europe he finds what he calls "international constitutionalism," in the United States "democratic constitutionalism." For Rubenfeld, the latter, American approach "sees constitutional law as the foundational law a particular polity has given itself through a special act of popular lawmaking," a constitution based on "deliberation and consent" which ultimately remains subject to the flexibility of politics. In contrast, for Rubenfeld, the former, European approach "sees constitutional law not as an act of democratic self-governance but as a check or restraint on democracy deriving its authority from its expression of universal rights and principles that transcend national boundaries," a constitution based on "reflection and choice" whose commitments stand above politics and can therefore be readily internationalized. Yet,

[22] On the different approaches to law generally in the US as compared to Europe, see Richard H. Pildes, "Conflicts between American and European Views of Law: The Dark Side of Legalism" (2003), 44 *Vanderbilt J Int L* 145, at 146–7.

[23] Jed Rubenfeld, "Unilateralism and Constitutionalism" (2004), 79 *NYULR* 1,971.

where Rubenfeld refers to constitutional values, others such as Kagan[24] and Delahunty[25] refer to political interests. John Ikenberry, in turn, refers to European attempts to make the dominant (US) power less threatening by "embedding that power in rules and institutions that channel and limit the ways that power is exercised."[26]

[24] Kagan, *Paradise and Power.*

[25] Delahunty, "The Battle of Mars and Venus."

[26] John Ikenberry, "Strategic Reactions to American Preeminence: Great Power Politics in the Age of Unipolarity," National Intelligence Council Conference Report (28 July 2003), available at www.cia.gov/nic/confreports__stratreact.htm (last visited 17 September 2007), at 14; see also Stephen M. Walt, *Taming American Power: The Global Response to U.S. Primacy* (New York: W. W. Norton, 2005), at 144–52.

3

Allocation, protection and back-up enforcement of entitlements

1 The basic model, its advantages and limitations

Although domestic law analogies are never fully appropriate, this book subjects international law to a framework that is well known in domestic US law, namely Calabresi and Melamed's 1972 distinction between inalienability, property rules and liability rules.[1] Although some scholars have previously referred to this model in discrete fields of international law,[2] this book is, to my knowledge, the first attempt to fully test the model for international law in general. What makes Calabresi and Melamed's model particularly interesting for international law is, first, that it

[1] Guido Calabresi and A. Douglas Melamed, "Property Rules, Liability Rules, and Inalienability: One View of the Cathedral" (1972), 85 *Harvard LR* 1,089. Many law review articles further specifying the model have followed. See, for example, Madeline Morris, "The Structure of Entitlements" (1993), 78 *Cornell LR* 822.

[2] See Jonathan Wiener, "Global Environmental Regulation: Instrument Choice in Legal Context" (1999), 108 *Yale LJ* 677; Warren Schwartz and Alan Sykes, "The Economic Structure of Renegotiation and Dispute Resolution in the World Trade Organization" (2002), 31 *J Leg Stud* 179; Joel P. Trachtman, "Building the WTO Cathedral" (2006), available at http://ssrn.com/abstract=815844; and Richard Morrison, "Efficient Breach of International Agreements" (1994), 23 *Denver J Int L Pol* 183.

offers a global matrix for legal entitlements, making abstraction of delineations deeply engrained in domestic law such as private versus public law, contract versus tort, civil versus criminal law. As international law does not formally uphold any of these distinctions,[3] such a simplified, global model is more attractive.

Secondly, the Calabresi and Melamed model uses the law and economics criteria of welfare maximization and rational action. As Sykes explained, "[p]ositive economic analysis of international legal regimes conventionally proceeds from an assumption that states behave as if they are rational maximizers over some set of preferences regarding the outcome of their interaction."[4] Transactions in

[3] The UN's International Law Commission (ILC) famously shelved a very controversial 1996 proposal (Draft Articles on State Responsibility (1996), Text of the Draft Articles Provisionally adopted by the Commission on first reading, UN Doc A/51/10, Report of the International Law Commission on the Work of its 48th Session, 58) to divide all internationally wrongful acts into, on the one hand, international crimes ("breach by a State of an international obligation so essential for the protection of fundamental interests of the international community that its breach is recognized as a crime by that community as a whole constitutes an international crime," Article 19.2) and, on the other hand, international delicts ("[a]ny internationally wrongful act which is not an international crime," Article 19.4). The final 2001 ILC Articles dropped the distinction between international crimes and international delicts but do attach special consequences to "serious breach by a State of an obligation arising under a peremptory norm of general international law" in Articles 40–41, discussed *infra* at pp. 187–8.

[4] Alan Sykes, "The Economics of Public International Law," John M. Olin Law and Economics Working Paper No. 216, July 2004, at 5.

international relations are thereby regarded as analogous to transactions in private markets, and the insights of economic tools applied to non-market circumstances. As Dunoff and Trachtman clarify, "[t]he assets traded in this international 'market' are not goods or services, but assets peculiar to states: components of power ... In international society, the equivalent of the market is simply the place where states interact to cooperate on particular issues – to trade in power – in order to maximize their baskets of preferences."[5] This "methodological individualism," on which law and economics rest, assumes that "each person [or state] is in charge of his or her own utility function and is a rational evaluative maximizer. It posits no values other than that of individual choice."[6]

When applying this approach to international law, several assumptions must be made, each of which translates into a specific critique or disadvantage of the method. First, to apply rational choice one must select a certain type or level of actor. For the purposes of this book, I select states. Yet, doing so, we must make abstraction of many intra-state dynamics and the role of non-state actors and individuals in the formation and enforcement of international law (I return to this critique below). Second, can international relations truly be reduced to market-type interactions where all that matters is money or price? Of course not. When law and economics use the terms welfare maximization and efficiency they are not limited to economic efficiency or monetary welfare. Instead,

[5] Jeffrey Dunoff and Joel Trachtman, "Economic Analysis of International Law" (1999), 24 *Yale J Int L* 1, at 13.

[6] *Ibid.*, at 11.

they refer to the maximization of an individual's or state's preferences, whatever these preferences may be (financial, moral, religious, geopolitical, etc.). The totality of these preferences is what is included in the so-called "utility function" of each actor. Yet, in some cases, it is impossible to put a value or price on certain preferences as they cannot be monetized. This is the critique of incommensurability which is further dealt with below. Third, can we really assume that states act in the overall interest of the entire population? Do they act rationally in the first place? Public choice theory tells us that the preferences of states may be assumed to be those of their political leaders. These leaders may maximize overall welfare, but may also seek to maximize votes, campaign contributions or their personal welfare. This, in turn, may mean that the interests of some sections of society are lifted above all others, even to the detriment of the nation's overall benefit.

All three sets of assumptions must be constantly remembered and limit the value of any economic analysis. However, with Sykes, this book takes the position that "the test is not whether the assumptions are fully descriptive of behavior, but whether they yield useful insights with empirical purchase."[7] Or as Krauss put it, "[a]nalysis of the choice between these types of rules [property versus liability rules] provides a useful purchase on the jurisprudential foundations of a legal system."[8] Indeed, if one assumes, for example,

[7] Sykes, "The Economics of Public International Law," at 6.

[8] Michael Krauss, "Property Rules vs. Liability Rules," in B. Bouckaert and G. De Geest (eds.), *Encyclopedia of Law and Economics* (Cheltenham: Edward Elgar, 1999), at 1.

that states do not act rationally, any attempt to describe or predict state behavior becomes, by definition, impossible and the scope for scholarly work of a normative nature all but evaporates. Although the rational actor model has its limitations and, as we shall see below, needs to be adapted to fit international law, the model offers a fresh departure from the increasingly subjective, almost ideological debate between supporters and critics of international law. This debate is too often based on predisposed positions for or against international law rather than an objective analysis of facts and incentives. In that sense, even if the Calabresi and Melamed model suffers from its own limitations, magnified as they are in international law, the model can and does offer new insights.

2 Step 1: allocation of entitlements

According to Calabresi and Melamed, the first issue which must be faced by any legal system is what they call the problem of "entitlement."[9] At the domestic level, a state is presented with the conflicting interests of two or more people, or groups of people, and must decide which side to favor. Does it grant an entitlement to make noise or an entitlement to have silence; an entitlement to private property or an entitlement to communal property; an entitlement to bodily integrity or an entitlement to rape or murder? Allocating an entitlement obviously has distributive effects, as it fixes the starting point

[9] Calabresi and Melamed, "Property Rules, Liability Rules, and Inalienability," at 1,090. The term "entitlement" is broader than the term "right," see *supra*, chapter 1 note 3.

for any subsequent transactions or transfers of entitlements. Equally, at the international level, rules of international law – and rulings by international tribunals – take sides in conflicts of interest between nations and, increasingly, between nations and individuals. Like domestic law, international treaties and custom allocate entitlements to pollute or to be free from pollution, entitlements to trade or to restrict trade, entitlements to non-intervention or to respect for human rights.

Crucially, however, whereas in domestic law the allocation of entitlements is achieved through state or other majoritarian regulation, in international law the traditional starting point is the sovereignty of individual states and the rule that a state's full entitlement over its territory and people can only be altered by that state's consent. From this perspective, international law is the prototype of a market-based, property rule regime: entitlements are only allocated or exchanged by consent. This raises the all-important question of attracting states to participate in a new rule or treaty, in particular when trying to tackle collective action problems such as global warming or nuclear proliferation. Without state consent to limit carbon emissions, for example, no state can be obliged to cut emissions. Since the consent rule also implies that states can, in principle, unilaterally withdraw from most of their commitments, preventing exit from treaties or other commitments is the second major problem in the allocation of international entitlements. Like the challenge of attracting participation, this risk of exit is not present in domestic legal systems. Indeed, within states, subjects cannot unilaterally exit from particular laws (other than through emigration and/or denouncing citizenship).

At the same time, even in international law the consent rule is not absolute and some elements of a central legislator are present, be it in the form of customary rules (which do not require the explicit consent of all states), UN Security Council Resolutions (which are binding on all UN members even when they object), references to the international community (in discussions on, for example, *jus cogens*), majority-based decisions by international organizations (like EU institutions) or, to some extent, compulsory jurisdiction of international tribunals (such as the WTO Appellate Body). All of these are examples where entitlements are allocated not merely by consent but through some higher or centralized authority, closer to the model Calabresi and Melamed had in mind when discussing domestic law.

3 Step 2: protection of entitlements

The *allocation* of entitlements raises the first order of legal decisions or what, in international law, are often referred to as primary rules. Having made its initial choice, the next question is how to *protect* that choice. Framed in the domestic context, once an entitlement is set to, for example, silence, private property or bodily integrity, the state must next decide how and how strongly to protect this entitlement. In such second-order decisions two questions must be answered.

First, can an individual sell or trade its entitlement? If not, the entitlement is said to be "inalienable." In most domestic legal systems, individuals cannot, for example, sell their kidneys or sell themselves into slavery even if they were willing to. Equally, minors cannot normally contract their entitlements away. This first type of entitlement is, in other words, immutable and non-transferable. It is, if you wish, written in stone unless and until it is altered by the legislator.

In case no such prohibition on transfer applies, the following, second question arises. For the entitlement to change hands, must the holder of the entitlement agree or can anyone simply take the entitlement and compensate for it? If the former is true – no one can take the entitlement unless the holder sells it willingly – the entitlement is said to be protected by a "property rule." You do not have the right, for example, to take possession of my house even if you pay the going rate for it. You can only have my house if I agree to sell it to you. This second type of entitlement is, in other words, one that can be transferred, traded or exchanged, but only with mutual consent. If the latter applies – the entitlement can be taken or destroyed for as long as compensation is paid – the entitlement is said to be protected by a "liability rule." The state can, for example, expropriate or take your land by eminent domain for as long as it pays you compensation. Equally, when an entitlement to clean air is protected by a pollution tax, I can unilaterally decide to pollute for as long as I pay the tax. This third type of entitlement is, in other words, one that can be bought off or taken unilaterally, subject only to a take-and-pay principle.

Applying these second-order concepts of inalienability, property rules and liability rules to international law, the following basic questions arise:

1 Can states freely transfer their entitlements under international law or should they at times be prohibited from

doing so (making the entitlements inalienable)? If so, when, why and how should such inalienability be imposed?

2 Can one state simply take or destroy the entitlement of another state, subject to compensation (liability rule or take-and-pay principle), or should certain entitlements only transfer if the holder willingly agrees (property rule or principle of mutual consent)? In other words, when, why and how should international law be protected by a property rule? And when, why and how should international law be protected by a mere liability rule?

There is no doubt, and Calabresi and Melamed openly admitted so,[10] that entitlements can be protected by hybrid regimes, such as combinations of property and liability protection, and that all three rules of protection come in different degrees. The same is true for international law. The Kyoto Protocol, for example, first imposes a collectively set cap on emissions for each committed country, a cap which parties cannot change *inter se* (reminiscent of inalienability).[11] Subsequently, however, the Kyoto Protocol allows parties to pollute above their ceiling for as long as they "pay" for it, either by buying emission credits from someone

[10] Calabresi and Melamed, "Property Rules, Liability Rules, and Inalienability," at 1,093 ("it should be clear that most entitlements to most goods are mixed. Taney's house may be protected by a property rule in situations where Marshall wishes to purchase it, by a liability rule where the government decides to take it by eminent domain, and by a rule of inalienability in situations where Taney is drunk or incompetent").

[11] Article 3, Kyoto Protocol to the United Nations Framework Convention on Climate Change, 11 December 1997, entry into force 16 February 2005.

else (consensual transfer suggestive of a property rule)[12] or by financing climate-friendly projects in developing countries under the so-called Clean Development Mechanism[13] (reminiscent of compensation under liability protection[14]). Equally, international entitlements can be made inalienable to different degrees. As discussed in chapter 5, peremptory norms of international law (*jus cogens*) are automatically binding on all states and super-inalienable as they cannot be transferred or contracted out from (unless the norm of *jus cogens* itself evolves). Yet, also treaties of a legislative type which set out collective obligations (such as human rights conventions) have inalienable features, albeit to a lesser extent than *jus cogens*: even if such obligations may only be binding on the parties who accepted them, they cannot be transferred or contracted out from *inter se* (that is, as between a sub-set of treaty members). Like inalienable entitlements under domestic criminal law, such collective entitlements can only be transferred or reallocated by the legislator itself (*in casu*, the collectivity of treaty parties).

[12] Article 6, Kyoto Protocol. [13] Article 12, Kyoto Protocol.

[14] But note that Kyoto parties can only take advantage of the Clean Development Mechanism (CDM) subject to certain eligibility requirements (such as annual reporting and the obligation to combine CDM credits with a minimum of domestic action to reduce emissions). In addition, not just any project in developing countries qualifies for the CDM. CDM projects must obtain the consent of the host developing country and be multilaterally approved by the CDM Executive Board. Yet, once a CDM project is approved it generates "certified emission credits" that a participant in the market can buy or trade. From this perspective, extra pollution can be bought off along the lines of liability protection. See http://cdm.unfccc.int/index.html (last visited 17 September 2007).

4 Step 3: back-up enforcement

What Calabresi and Melamed only addressed in passing, however, is that a legal system cannot rest once it has answered the second-order question of how to protect entitlements. Indeed, a third and final question logically follows, namely: what happens if someone takes or destroys an entitlement *against* the rules? Put differently, how does the state respond when murder does occur, when you take my house *without* my agreement or when I pollute but refuse to pay the pollution tax? Whereas the first two steps of allocation and protection of entitlements deal with the *intra*-contractual questions of who originally gets the entitlement and how can it be exchanged, the third step of back-up enforcement moves to the *extra*-contractual question of what happens in case someone does not follow the contractual agreement.

That Calabresi and Melamed did not examine this third-order question of back-up enforcement in any detail is easily understood. In domestic law, the state has a monopoly on the use of coercive force and a variety of instruments in hand to compel its subjects to comply with the rules. Depending on how and how strongly it decided to protect entitlements (step 2), a state can simply tailor-make appropriate forms of back-up enforcement (step 3): it can seize my property when I refuse to pay a pollution tax; it can issue court injunctions and fine or even incarcerate you for occupying my house; and it can imprison, or even execute, the murderer. Given that all of these options are readily available in domestic law, Calabresi and Melamed did not give much attention to back-up enforcement.

Under international law, of course, the situation is different. In the absence of central enforcement, states cannot be jailed, let alone be executed. Moreover, when states refuse to pay compensation most of their property is protected by sovereign immunity. This means that in international law the third-order question of what happens if entitlements are taken against the rules deserves attention. For many observers, it even becomes crucial. However, as scholarship on compliance in international law demonstrates, even at the international level compliance is the norm, not the exception.[15] Although it does not normally come about through centralized enforcement (as in domestic law), in most cases it is induced through reciprocity, retaliation, reputation and/or the normative pull, legitimacy or consent-based nature of international obligations themselves. In other words, the difference between back-up enforcement in domestic as opposed to international law is not that in the former there is back-up enforcement, and in the latter there is none. Instead, the difference is one in nature or quality, not necessarily degree or quantity.

As a result, one of the core arguments of this book is that also in international law it is useful to distinguish the second step of setting the desired level of protection of entitlements from the third step of sanctions or back-up enforcement in case the rules are not respected. What this book advocates is that treaty negotiators first make an objective decision on the optimal level of protection of entitlements pursuant to the matrix developed below (step 2: inalienability, property or liability protection) and then, based on that

[15] See *supra*, Introduction notes 1–7.

decision, calibrate appropriate sanctions or back-up enforcement to address extra-contractual behavior (step 3). Similarly, as further explained below in chapter 6, given the non-conventional incentives that induce compliance with international law (ranging from reputation and reciprocity to normative pull and community pressure), it is misleading to reverse-engineer the level of protection for a certain entitlement (step 2) based on what the treaty provides in terms of back-up enforcement (step 3). For example, the mere fact that the remedy for breach of a treaty obligation is compensation or 1:1 retaliation does not mean that the entitlement is protected by a liability rule. The compensation can, indeed, be the "price" for taking an entitlement under a liability regime; but it can also be the "sanction" for breach, in which case the entitlement can be said to be protected by a property rule. The same mistake can be made in domestic law: the mere fact that the remedy for contract breach is damages does not mean that contracts are protected by a liability rule; in some cases, the damages can simply be a "price" (in which case we can speak of liability protection); in other cases, it can be a "sanction" (part of property protection).

5 A framework for the protection of international law entitlements

In sum, rather than asking the tired question of whether international law is law or legally binding, the framework proposed in this book is three-pronged:

1 Allocation: how does international law allocate entitlements?

2 Protection: how does international law protect entitlements?
3 Back-up enforcement: what happens if international rules of protection are disregarded?

Crucially, within the second prong of protection, three broad possibilities arise:

1 make the entitlement inalienable
2 protect it as property, making its transfer subject to mutual consent
3 protect the entitlement under a mere liability rule or take-and-pay principle.

This model also provides an alternative to, and is arguably more sophisticated than, the one adopted by the International Law Commission in its 2001 Articles on State Responsibility. There, the ILC, as most international lawyers do, bifurcates all of international law between, on the one hand, primary rules which "define the content of . . . international obligations, the breach of which gives rise to responsibility" and, on the other hand, secondary rules which address "the general conditions under international law for the State to be considered responsible for wrongful actions or omissions, and the legal consequences which flow therefrom."[16]

While focusing on the second order question of how international law protects entitlements (through inalienability, property rules or liability rules), a crucial point of this book is

[16] United Nations, Draft Articles on Responsibility of States for Internationally Wrongful Acts, with commentaries 2001 (2008) available at http://untreaty.un.org/ilc/texts/instruments/english/commentaries/9_6_2001.pdf, at 31.

that, at the international level, any such attempt must be made in context. First, we must take account of the *preceding* step of how international law allocates entitlements (essentially through voluntary assent which creates the dual problem of attracting participation and preventing exit). Secondly, we cannot lose sight of the *next* step of how international law responds, or can respond, when entitlements are taken against the rules (non-centralized back-up enforcement).

In addition, the underlying reason for why a specific allocation was agreed upon in step 1 can have important consequences also for the optimal design of the treaty in steps 2 and 3. If, for example, a treaty is concluded in step 1 to address a so-called prisoners' dilemma or cooperation problem, where high incentives exist to defect (such as, according to most observers, the original GATT[17]), optimal levels of protection and enforcement under steps 2 and 3 are likely to differ as compared to a treaty concluded with the aim of solving an assurance or coordination game, where there are fewer incentives to defect (such as, according to some observers,[18]

[17] WTO Secretariat, World Trade Report (2007), at 50.

[18] See, for example, Brian Langille, "Core Labour Rights – The True Story (Reply to Alston)" (2005), 16 *European J Int L* 409, at 419: "Briefly, on the old, familiar . . . view, the role of the ILO is to provide legal rules, and a mechanism for 'enforcing' them, aimed at preventing member states from making the economically rational move of trading off lower labour standards in order to secure economic benefits [that is, a prisoners' dilemma situation] . . . [a] better account depends most basically upon a richer . . . account of the relationship between social justice and economic progress . . . on this view social justice (including labour rights) is both the goal of, and the precondition to, the creation of durable economies and societies. The role of the ILO is not to block through some

ILO conventions).[19] In terms of back-up enforcement, the prisoners' dilemma situation may require sanctions to reduce the chances of defection; in the assurance game, a more managerial approach of information exchange, capacity-building and positive incentives may be more appropriate. Similarly, where entitlements are allocated in step 1 on a reciprocal basis between (sets of) two states (as in bilateral trade agreements or the original GATT), market-based property protection pursuant to which the entitlement can be exchanged or, depending on the circumstances, a liability rule where entitlements can be taken subject to compensation, may be appropriate. If, in contrast, the entitlement was allocated on a non-reciprocal basis in pursuit of collective interests that transcend bilateral state-to-state interests and relationships (as is the case for most human rights conventions), a form of inalienability protection may be more appropriate.

If international law is to further develop and refine, it must not merely attempt to create more rules (first-order decisions), nor stare itself blind at the lack of centralized enforcement (third-order decisions). It must incorporate the second-order nuances of variable protection common in domestic law and justified *a fortiori* at the international level. Indeed, as further developed below, my claim is that at the

legally binding agreement and legal 'enforcement' mechanism the member states from pursuing their individual self-interest, but rather to help member states see where their self-interest actually lies and to assist them in getting there [that is, an assurance game]."

[19] Vinod Aggarwal and Cédric Dupont, "Collaboration and Coordination in the Global Political Economy," in John Ravenhill (ed.), *Global Political Economy* (Oxford: Oxford University Press, 2004).

international level there are *additional* reasons, not present (or not to the same degree) in domestic law, to stop short of making all entitlements inalienable. By clinging to what they regard as the legal nirvana of immutable international law, European absolutists and other traditional supporters of international law overlook that even in domestic law most entitlements must *not* be sacredly respected. Even with the full force of centralized enforcement available, domestic law deliberately chooses to permit the contracting away of most entitlements (that is, those protected by a property rule). In addition, in a growing number of regulatory fields – including, in particular, environmental protection – domestic law goes as far as allowing the unilateral taking of entitlements subject only to compensation (thus protecting entitlements by a mere liability rule). In the context of environmental protection, for example, Wiener writes that after thirty years of debate and experience, analysts agree that "incentive-based instruments such as taxes and tradable allowances should generally be chosen over technology requirements and fixed emissions standards because the incentive-based instruments are typically far more cost-effective and innovation-generating than their alternatives." Moreover, "among the incentive instruments, the price-based tax and liability rule instruments – which set a price on emissions and let sources adjust the quantity they emit – will typically be superior to the quantity-based tradable allowance and property rule instruments – which set the quantity of emissions and let the sources bargain over price."[20]

[20] Wiener, "Global Environmental Regulation," at 682. On the benefits of liability rules over property rules in terms of technological innovation

Most importantly, domestic legal systems permit such compensated takings not for lack of enforcement tools, but because they regard such lower levels of protection as more effective and efficient. In that sense, when setting the uniform target of inalienability, European absolutists try to be "more catholic than the pope." Their paradoxical over-ambition in the face of obvious weakness begs for criticism. By setting a standard that it cannot and, more importantly, *should not* always meet, international law would further undermine its already precarious credibility.[21] Indeed, as discussed later (chapter 6.2), inalienability in international law as it is currently constructed risks leading to less, rather than more, compliance and enforcement.

In response to American voluntarists and other critics of international law, the nuanced framework proposed in this book demonstrates that the absence of an immutable and centrally enforced international law does not undermine international law's claim to normativity. Not because international law, in the absence of centralized enforcement, ought to lower its expectations, but because the normativity of international law, much like that of domestic law, comes in degrees. As in domestic law, in international law as well, it is often times more efficient and appropriate to protect

for certain areas now covered by intellectual property rights, see Jerome Reichmann, "Of Green Tulips and Legal Kudzu: Repackaging Rights in Subpatentable Innovation" (2000), 53 *Vanderbilt LR* 1743.

[21] As Sophocles famously noted: "What you cannot enforce, do not command" (Sophocles, Greek tragic dramatist [496–406 BC], see www.quotationspage.com/quote/2664.html, last visited 17 September 2007).

entitlements by a property or liability rule rather than by strict inalienability. Moreover, as elaborated below, sanctions and centralized enforcement are not the only – nor probably the most important – reasons why states, even individuals within states, comply with law. Their absence or relative weakness in the international context does not, therefore, render international law irrelevant; nor does it obviate further refinements between allocation, protection and back-up enforcement. On the contrary, as demonstrated below (chapter 6.1), it is exactly the level of protection of international law entitlements (e.g., are they protected by a liability or a property rule?) that sets and triggers the level of what I will call "community costs," and it is those costs that are, in turn, crucial to achieve compliance with international law. Put differently, international law itself, in particular by setting the level of protection of entitlements and thereby calibrating reputation and other "community costs," influences the incentives for states to comply and, thereby, state behavior. From this perspective, state preferences are not purely exogenous or simply "a given"; they are influenced by international law and institutions through interaction on the basis of shared legal norms and expectations.[22]

[22] This is a central tenet of the so-called "constructivist" school. See John Ruggie, *Constructing the World Polity: Essays on International Institutionalization* (London: Routledge, 1998).

4

How should international law entitlements be protected?

This chapter tackles the core normative question of how international entitlements *ought to be* protected under the second prong of this book's three-pronged framework (allocation, protection, back-up enforcement). It first explains why in domestic law, and also in international law, property protection should be the default form of protection of entitlements unless special circumstances arise (section 1). As a result, what I have called European absolutism (in favor of hard inalienability) and American voluntarism (in favor of simple liability protection) are both undesirable extremes. Subsequently, I describe the circumstances in which deviation from the default rule of property protection may be advisable, first toward stronger protection of entitlements as inalienable (section 2), second toward weaker protection of entitlements under a liability rule (section 3). Yet, for both types of deviation from the default rule of property protection, I discuss a number of important caveats: section 4 sums up elements that, where present in, for example, a specific treaty context, favor *weaker* protection of international law; section 5, in contrast, offers features that militate for *stronger* protection of international law. Chapter 4 concludes with a matrix that summarizes the criteria that treaty negotiators should consider when selecting the optimal level of protection for a new treaty or other rule of international law. Chapter 5 tests these normative predictions to the current state of protection of international law entitlements.

1 The argument for a default rule of property protection

Implied in the Calabresi and Melamed model is that, in domestic law at least, property protection should be the default rule. In other words, once allocated, entitlements should be freely tradable unless there are either (1) solid reasons to stop or prevent such trading by making the entitlement inalienable, or (2) good excuses to stimulate or force a beneficial transfer that would otherwise not occur (or at too high a price) by protecting the entitlement under a mere liability rule. This "free market" of entitlements flows naturally from the law and economics analogy with transactions in private markets and its underlying methodological individualism which assumes that each person is in charge of his or her utility function and maximizes its preferences through private trades.[1] Should international law have a

[1] From a domestic law perspective, Paul Epstein, for example, has pointed out that "[t]he standard practice in virtually all legal systems assumes the dominance of property rules . . . everywhere and in every society property rules form the norm and liability rules the crucial exception": Paul Epstein, "A Clear View of *The Cathedral*: The Dominance of Property Rules" (1996), 106 *Yale LJ* 2,091, at 2,092 and 2,096. Alan Schwartz as well has argued in favor of specific performance as the default rule on the ground that information problems about valuation, enforcement, and so forth, are always present: Alan Schwartz, "The Case for Specific Performance" (1979), 89 *Yale LJ* 271. See also Daniel Friedmann, "The Efficient Breach Fallacy" (1989), 18 *J Leg Stud* 1, at

similar default preference for property protection where trades are freely permitted? Two reasons support an answer in the affirmative: the first is an extrapolation from domestic law (contractual freedom and welfare maximization); the second is specific to the international law context (property protection requires the least amount of intervention).

(a) *Contractual freedom and welfare maximization*

The core reason for a default rule of property protection is individual freedom and the maximization of welfare that it should, in principle, bring about. The individual him- or herself, not the state or some other centralized power, is best suited to value his or her needs and preferences (both pecuniary and non-pecuniary). As a result, letting individuals decide for themselves whether, and on what terms, to transfer entitlements should, in principle, lead to the maximization of individual as well as overall welfare. Put differently, to transfer an entitlement to the one who values it the most ensures the most efficient allocation of resources.

This basic *rationale* for contractual freedom and property protection is readily transposable to international law. Indeed, if anything, in the inter-state context, it applies with even greater force. Given the enormous political,

13–14: "The efficient breach theory is in fundamental conflict with a basic premise of both the common law and other Western legal systems, namely, that property (including contractual rights) is not be taken and given to another without the owner's consent. There are few exceptions to this principle. The major one is in public law [the government's power of eminent domain]."

economic and social diversity between states, and in the absence of a socially cohesive world community, states themselves, not international institutions or some form of world government, are, in principle, best suited to value state preferences. To let states decide on when, and on what terms, to transfer their entitlements should, in principle, maximize inter-state welfare and ensure the most efficient allocation of resources.[2] If two states want to change an earlier treaty or agree to settle a dispute, even in a way that is inconsistent with an earlier treaty, why stop them (through inalienability)? Equally, if a state holder of an entitlement values its entitlement more than what a potential buyer is willing to offer for it (and no transfer occurs), why attempt to objectively value the entitlement and force a transfer (through liability protection)? If a potential buyer truly attaches higher value to the entitlement than the current holder does, should a transfer not occur naturally, without forcing the hand of the seller? In domestic law, state intervention either prohibiting transfer (inalienability) or forcing the transfer of individual entitlements (liability) can be justified on majoritarian terms. In the international context, however, there is no global democracy and a huge diversity between states. Hence, centralized intervention is more difficult (though, of course, not impossible) to justify internationally than nationally. In sum, both in domestic and *a fortiori* in international law, principles of freedom and welfare maximization (to avoid the notion of state sovereignty)

[2] Below I question whether this process necessarily achieves maximization of intra-state welfare.

militate in favor of a default rule of property protection. Indeed, as noted earlier, the consent-based nature of allocation of entitlements under traditional international law (step 1) offers the prototype background for a market-based system of property protection (under step 2).

(b) Property protection requires less intervention

Although contractual freedom and welfare maximization are sufficient reasons, in both domestic and international law, for the default rule of property protection, there is an additional argument specific to international law: as compared to both inalienability and liability protection, protecting entitlements as property gives rise to the least amount of intervention. Since an entitlement protected by property rule can be freely traded between a willing buyer and a willing seller, property protection "lets each of the parties say how much the entitlement is worth to him, and gives the seller a veto if the buyer does not offer enough."[3] In other words, the transfer of entitlements is simply left to voluntary negotiations. Call it the market place of entitlements. No centralized power is required either to prohibit transfers (as in inalienability) or to objectively valuate entitlements that were unilaterally taken (as in liability protection). Since international law generally lacks centralized law-making and enforcement, the level of protection

[3] Guido Calabresi and A. Douglas Melamed, "Property Rules, Liability Rules, and Inalienability: One View of the Cathedral" (1972), 85 *Harvard LR* 1,089, at 1,092.

with the least amount of intervention is logically best suited. Indeed, if we make an international entitlement inalienable, who will ensure that it is, in practice, not transferred or violated? Equally, when we let states unilaterally take entitlements or breach treaties for as long as they pay compensation, who will objectively determine the appropriate level of compensation and make sure that, afterwards, compensation is actually paid? Although property protection also needs intervention (i.e., who will make sure that entitlements are not taken without consent?), none is needed at the stage of transfer (unlike under a liability rule where collective valuation is required), and at the back-up enforcement stage less intervention is required for property protection (only the absence of consent must be controlled) as opposed to inalienability (where even transfers by consent must be stopped). That said, the question of how a decentralized system like international law backs up a property regime does remain, and is discussed in chapter 6 below.

2 When to protect entitlements as inalienable

If reasons of contractual freedom, welfare maximization and degree of intervention favor a default rule of property protection in international law – or, put differently, militate *against* European absolutism or inalienability across the board – under what circumstances should entitlements nonetheless be protected as inalienable? In other words, when should states be prevented from transferring entitlements or changing treaties or custom even *with* mutual consent?

The starting point for any discussion on inalienability, be it in domestic or international law, is this: anyone who believes in individual freedom, or the freedom of states to set their own destiny, ought to be wary of setting norms in stone, that is, of making entitlements inalienable. Once labeled as inalienable neither individuals (under domestic law) nor states (under international law) can transfer the entitlement. That is not to say that no entitlement ought to be inalienable, only that the criteria for inalienability need to be carefully scrutinized. As discussed below, this is, however, not the case in international law. For Calabresi and Melamed, in contrast, who address inalienability in domestic law, inalienability can be appropriate on three grounds: significant externalities, moralisms and paternalism.[4]

(a) Significant externalities

Under the Calabresi and Melamed model, inalienability may be called for in cases where the transfer of the entitlement would create such significant externalities – that is, costs to third parties (as in pollution) – that no buyer would be willing to pay for them. In that case, "setting up the machinery for collective valuation will be wasteful" and "[b]arring the sale [of, for example, land] to polluters will be the most efficient result because it is clear that avoiding pollution is cheaper than paying its costs – including the

4 For a more detailed analysis of inalienability, see Susan Rose-Ackerman, "Inalienability and the Theory of Property Rights" (1985), 85 *Columbia LR* 931.

costs to [third parties]."[5] Put differently, as the transfer cannot increase welfare, it is best to ban it.

Applied to international law, a first reason to make an entitlement inalienable is, therefore, that its transfer necessarily creates costs that exceed any possible benefit. If states agree, for example, not to use certain weapons, thereby allocating an entitlement to be free from the harm caused by these weapons, states could also ban any subsequent agreement that allows a country to use the weapon even if that country is willing to pay for it. The reason to do so could then be that the harm caused by the weapon necessarily exceeds any benefit to be gained by the weapon-using country. Put differently, where an activity would create such high degree of externalities – say, dropping a nuclear bomb or wide-scale, cross-border pollution – no one might be willing or able to pay for all the costs related to the transfer of the entitlement. Hence, it may be more efficient to ban the transfer in the first place.

(b) Moralisms and incommensurability

A second reason for inalienability is, according to Calabresi and Melamed, based on so-called moralisms or values. In some cases "external costs do not lend themselves to collective measurement which is acceptably objective and nonarbitrary."[6] In theory, one could value the external costs to other people in society related to my willingly selling

[5] Calabresi and Melamed, "Property Rules, Liability Rules, and Inalienability," at 1,111.

[6] *Ibid.*, at 1,112.

myself into slavery and force the buyer to pay not just me, but also all third parties whose morals would be harmed by seeing me as a slave. Yet, because we feel that any monetization of, for example, freedom or a kidney is, by hypothesis, out of the question, most states decided to make the entitlement to be free from slavery, or to our kidneys, inalienable.

This objection of moralisms later developed into what is now referred to as the problem of incommensurability.[7] Under this heading, critics of the broader law and economics approach point out that to ask for the economic value of certain social goods is to make a category error.[8] Another variant argues that, while it may be possible to calculate economic trade-offs between different goods, to understand trade-offs simply in economic terms is to "do violence" to our understandings of these goods.[9] A third critique grounded in the incommensurability thesis submits that by comparing diverse goods in economic terms we transform our understanding of these goods in objectionable ways: we commodify these goods and thereby debase them.[10]

Applied to international law, a second reason to make an entitlement inalienable is, therefore, that the

[7] See Jeffrey Dunoff and Joel Trachtman, "Economic Analysis of International Law" (1999), 24 *Yale J Int L* 1, at 48; and Jane Baron and Jeffrey Dunoff, "Against Market Rationality: Moral Critiques of Economic Analysis in Legal Theory" (1996), 17 *Cardozo LR* 431.

[8] See Mark Sagoff, "Economic Theory and Environmental Law" (1981), 79 *Michigan LR* 1,393, at 1,411.

[9] See Cass Sunstein, "Incommensurability and Valuation in Law" (1994), 92 *Michigan LR* 779.

[10] See Margaret Jane Radin, "Market Inalienability" (1987), 100 *Harvard LR* 1,849, at 1,850.

entitlement relates to a universal or quasi-universal moral value (such as the prohibition of slavery or apartheid) which makes any monetized transfer, by definition, impossible or inappropriate. International law could then allocate inalienable entitlements against, for example, slavery, genocide, aggression and crimes against humanity on the ground that states consider it inappropriate to monetize the values protected by these norms. In other words, where it is difficult, if not impossible, to put a price on an entitlement (to, for example, freedom or the survival of an ethnic group), it makes sense to ban the transfer of that entitlement altogether.

(c) Paternalism

A third reason to protect entitlements as inalienable (other than high externalities and incommensurability) is, according to Calabresi and Melamed, paternalism. They distinguish between self-paternalism and true paternalism. Self-paternalism explains why Ulysses tied himself to the mast, or why individuals pass a bill of rights or constitutional safeguards "so that they will be prevented from yielding to momentary temptations which they deem harmful to themselves."[11] The same logic applies when making invalid contracts entered into when drunk or under undue influence or coercion. True paternalism, in turn, explains why we prohibit a whole range of activities by minors.

[11] Calabresi and Melamed, "Property Rules, Liability Rules, and Inalienability," at 1,113.

Applied to international law, states may find reasons to tie their hands to the mast of a certain international norm so as to avoid future temptations to deviate from such norm, or limit contracting in situations of duress or coercion (self-paternalism). They may also consider it necessary to limit the transfer of entitlements held by states in situations of particular weakness (true paternalism).

3 When to protect entitlements under a liability rule

With the earlier arguments in favor of property protection as the default rule – contractual freedom, welfare maximization and degree of intervention all required militating as much against American voluntarism (liability) as against European absolutism (inalienability) – why would we ever expect a legal system to move away from property protection, or the free market exchange of entitlements, in favor of unilateral takings under a liability rule? The answer, in short, is: to correct market failure. In the previous section, I discussed reasons to make entitlements inalienable (significant externalities, incommensurability and paternalism). Inalienability favors the *holder* of an entitlement: even if the holder *wants* to sell the entitlement, he or she is not permitted to do so. Inalienability *prevents* trading. At the other extreme of inalienability, one may also deviate from property protection by imposing a mere liability rule. Liability protection favors the *taker* of an entitlement: even where the holder does *not* agree to transfer the entitlement, anyone can unilaterally take the entitlement on the sole condition that the holder gets compensated (take-and-pay principle). Rather than preventing trade, liability protection *stimulates* or even *forces* trade.

Yet, in international law, why should we ever permit a state to unilaterally take the entitlement of another state *without* that state's consent? At this stage, it is useful to revert to the reasons offered by Calabresi and Melamed for liability protection in domestic law. They offer three reasons to replace property by liability protection: hold-out, free-load and high transaction costs. The first two are also referred to as strategic behavior.

(a) Hold-out

Even where the sale of entitlements is welfare enhancing (that is, the buyer values the entitlement higher than the seller), certain sellers, or holders of the entitlement, may refuse to sell at the normal price in the hope of capturing more of the premium that the buyers are willing to pay. In other words, entitlement *holders* may engage in strategic behavior. Calabresi and Melamed use the example of eminent domain where owners of land may hold out in order to get a higher price from the town authority wanting to build a park. Even though objectively the park is Pareto desirable (that is, the town's citizens value a park more than the land-owners value their land), with enough hold-outs, the park will not be built. Liability protection resolves this hold-out problem so as to achieve the most efficient outcome: "If society can remove from the market the valuation of each tract of land, decide the value collectively, and impose it, then the hold-out problem is gone."[12] In other words, under a liability rule or take-and-pay principle, the town can simply take the land and compensate its owners at an objectively determined value. As pointed out earlier, whereas property protection, with its market place of entitlements, reflects Adam Smith's invisible hand or liberal capitalism, liability protection corresponds to social interventionism. It is, therefore, no small irony that liability protection, the quest for efficient breach and what I have called American voluntarism – each of which implies a high degree of intervention for the collective good – are generally advocated in politically conservative circles, including the law and economics school.

Under international law, it is easy to think of similar hold-out problems for which a liability rule may offer a solution. If, for example, the EC wants to renegotiate one of its tariff commitments in the WTO treaty and the EC is perfectly willing to pay each WTO member for this change (e.g., with a tariff reduction on other products), some WTO members may hold out. That is, they may refuse to sign the amendment even though they are, objectively, offered full compensation (e.g., they get a lower tariff on some other product). Why so? Because in such renegotiation, especially with 152 parties involved, WTO members – who, of course, realize that the proposed amendment is apparently important for the EC – have an incentive to hide their true valuation so as to extract ever more compensation from the EC. With enough hold-outs, the price requested from the EC

[12] *Ibid.*, at 1,107.

may simply kill the deal, even though objectively it should have materialized. In this situation, the market (*in casu* consensual renegotiation of the WTO treaty) fails to establish what is Pareto desirable. Moving from a property rule (which requires consent from all sides) to a liability rule (where entitlements can be taken unilaterally as long as compensation is paid) can then offer a way out. Under such a liability regime, or take-and-pay principle, the EC could then simply increase its tariff but pay other WTO members for it, at an objectively set level, either by offering trade compensation or by suffering trade retaliation. As discussed below, this is exactly the liability regime that Article XXVIII of GATT (tariff renegotiations) and Article XXI of GATS (renegotiation of specific commitments in services trade) provide for. In a recent WTO dispute where the Appellate Body found that a US ban on internet gambling violates US market access commitments under GATS, the United States has, for example, renegotiated its GATS commitments with, among others, the EU (thereby offering the EU trade compensation) rather than bringing its legislation into compliance.[13] In its relations with those WTO members that cannot agree with such renegotiation, the US can decide to keep the ban but to suffer retaliation, either under GATS Article XXI procedures themselves or as a remedy under the WTO dispute settlement system. The latter option was exercised by the original complainant in this dispute, Antigua and

[13] See Inside US Trade, "U.S., EU Settle On Gambling Compensation; U.S. Faces Legal Questions," 21 December 2007, available at www.insidetrade.com/secure/dsply_nl_txt.asp?f=wto2002.ask&dh=100298957&q=gambling.

Barbuda, who obtained WTO authorization to retaliate against the US to the tune of US$21 million per year.[14]

(b) Free-load

Besides hold-out, Calabresi and Melamed offer the problem of free-load or free-riders as a second reason to move from property to liability protection. While hold-out represents strategic behavior by sellers (or entitlement holders), free-load is strategic behavior by buyers (that is, potential takers of the entitlement). Going back to the example of eminent domain and the building of a park, although the town's citizens may each value the land at a price that makes the sale Pareto desirable, some citizens (i.e., potential buyers) may try to free-load. That is, they may claim that the park is only worth $50 to them or even nothing at all (instead of the true value to them of, say, $100). They would, of course, do so in the hope that other citizens will chip in more and buy the land with their money, even though subsequently everyone would benefit from the park. With enough free-loaders unwilling to pay, the park may not materialize even though it is Pareto desirable.

[14] See *United States – Measures Affecting the Cross-Border Supply of Gambling and Betting Services*, Recourse to Arbitration by the United States under DSU Article 22.6, WT/DS285/ARB, 21 December 2007. Yet Antigua, in addition, also requested compensation under GATS Article XXI, see Inside US Trade, "Antigua, Costa Rica Request Arbitration On Gambling Compensation," 1 February 2008, available at www.insidetrade.com/secure/dsply_nl_txt.asp?f=wto2002.ask&dh=103431524&q=gambling.

As with the hold-out problem, liability protection may then offer a way out: "if society can value collectively each individual citizen's desire to have a park and charge him a 'benefits' tax based upon it, the freeloader problem is gone. If the sum of the taxes is greater than the sum of the compensation awards, the park will result."[15] Put differently, where the entitlement of citizens to their money is protected by mere liability, the town can simply take the citizens' money (that is, impose a tax) and compensate them with the creation of a park.

Moving now to international law, it is readily apparent that the largely consensual nature of international law-making – that is, states *cannot* normally be forced into an international norm or scheme without their consent – severely limits the way international law can deal with free-loaders. If a state decides to free-load, for example, on the commitments made by other countries to cut emissions under the Kyoto Protocol or to stop the trade in conflict diamonds, there is, in principle, nothing that international law can do to force these free-loaders to join the Kyoto Protocol or to participate in the Kimberley Scheme. In the absence of centralized power, no one can, for example, force the United States or China to impose an emissions tax. The only two things that existing Kyoto Protocol members can do is to either lure or force non-parties into joining with the use of, respectively, carrots or sticks. The former process of using carrots has been referred to by Wiener as the

[15] Calabresi and Melamed, "Properly Rules, Liability Rules, and Inalienability," at 1,107.

"beneficiary pays" principle (instead of the traditional "polluter pays" principle): given the inability to impose treaties on states against their will (especially those that pollute the most and have the clearest incentive to free-ride), somewhat ironically, it is often up to the beneficiaries or strongest proponents of the treaty (who may not be the biggest polluters) to "pay" potential free-riders to join (including the biggest polluters).[16] Such payment can be monetary, in the form of capacity building or transfer of technology, or by means of lesser commitments for potential free-riders that agree to join. Alternatively, the use of sticks, or economic or other pressure, to force participation of free-riders in international regimes can be seen, for example, in the OECD's scheme against money-laundering, the so-called Financial Action Task Force (FATF).[17] The FATF issued a list of forty recommendations to fight money-laundering and gave itself the mandate to monitor compliance with those recommendations (including the imposition of sanctions), even by states that did not join the scheme. No surprise, therefore, that FATF can proudly state on its website that "[d]uring 1991 and 1992, the FATF expanded its membership from the original 16 to 28 members." Similarly, the Montreal Protocol on Substances that Deplete the Ozone Layer, in its Article 4.1, imposes an obligation on all parties to ban the import of controlled substances from any *non*-party, thereby providing a clear incentive to non-parties to join the

[16] Jonathan Wiener, "Global Environmental Regulation: Instrument Choice in Legal Context" (1999), 108 *Yale LJ* 677, at 750.

[17] See www.fatf-gafi.org (last visited 17 September 2007).

Montreal Protocol.[18] The Kimberley Scheme on Conflict Diamonds (chapter III(c)) equally calls upon participants to "ensure that no shipment of rough diamonds is imported from or exported to a non-Participant." As a result, the number of participants in the scheme continues to grow.

Given the consent rule and the general absence of rule-making or taxation by fiat or majoritarian decision in international affairs, one would, therefore, predict that at least one of the traditional reasons offered in domestic law in favor of liability rules (namely, free-load) is hard to apply in international law.[19] The solution of using carrots or sticks to induce free-riders to join a treaty regime, as referred to in the examples above, at the end of the day, leads to the consensual joining of the free-rider, a feature of property protection.

(c) *High transaction costs*

A third reason that Calabresi and Melamed offer to shift from property to liability protection is not strategic behavior by either seller (hold-out) or buyer (free-load) but high, or even prohibitive, transaction costs. The famous

[18] As of July 2006, Ratification of the Montreal Protocol increased from 29 at its entry into force to 189 as of July 2006 (see http://ozone.unep.org/Treaties_and_Ratification/2C_ratificationTable.asp).

[19] This point was made earlier by Wiener, "Global Environmental Regulation," at 683 ("the presumption favoring environmental taxes depends on the assumptions that the regulator can compel polluters to comply by fiat and that the regulator can impose the instrument directly on polluters without an intermediate level of government in the way. But neither of these assumptions – coercive fiat or unitary regulation – is valid in the global legal context").

Coase Theorem tells us that, in the absence of transaction costs, parties will bargain to mutual advantage and renegotiate or transfer entitlements to achieve the most efficient outcome irrespective of how the legal system originally allocated the entitlements.[20] In reality, of course, transaction costs and asymmetries of information do exist and often prevent efficient transfers. This means, first, that the first step of allocating entitlements does matter and, second, that where transaction costs are high, thereby preventing welfare-enhancing transfers, intervention in the market may be required (through, for example, liability protection).

Calabresi and Melamed give the example of accidents and how it would be extremely expensive, if not prohibitive, to protect a victim's entitlement not to be accidentally injured as property. Indeed, in that case, anyone who engages in activities that may injure others would have to negotiate with all potential victims and buy the right, for example, "to knock off an arm or a leg."[21] Such requirement would preclude most activities that involve risk, even though these activities may, from an overall-welfare perspective, be worth having (ranging from driving cars to using certain machinery or new technologies). Much like hold-outs and free-loads, the problem of high transaction costs can be resolved through liability protection. As Calabresi and Melamed note, "perhaps the most common [reason], for employing a liability rule rather than a property rule to protect an entitlement is that market

[20] Ronald Coase, "The Problem of Social Cost" (1960), 3 *JL Econ* 1.

[21] Calabresi and Melamed, "Property Rules, Liability Rules, and Inalienability," at 1,109.

valuation of the entitlement is deemed inefficient, that is, it is either unavailable or too expensive compared to a collective valuation."[22] Hence, instead of forcing risk-takers to *ex ante* negotiate a deal with all potential victims (or to *ex ante* ban or limit risky but generally welfare-enhancing activities), in domestic law, the entitlement of people to be free from accidental injury is protected *ex post* by a liability rule. As a result, the risk-taker can take the entitlement (i.e., accidentally cause harm) but will then have to compensate the victim.

In sum, as Dunoff and Trachtman pointed out, "property rules may be used to promote efficient exchange where transaction costs are low, while liability rules may be appropriate where transaction costs are high."[23]

Should high or prohibitive transaction costs be a common reason to protect international entitlements under a liability rule? In one sense (low number of states), transaction costs under international law could be expected to be lower. As there are, after all, only 191 states and only so many neighboring countries for each state, it is, in many cases, possible to have *ex ante* negotiations with all potential victims. In contrast, when, for example, driving a car under domestic law the number of potential victims runs in the thousands, if not millions, and *ex ante* negotiations are virtually impossible. Under UNCLOS, for example, any state party that wants to change the rules (that is, "buy" certain entitlements from other members) will, indeed, need to

[22] *Ibid.*, at 1,110.

[23] Dunoff and Trachtman, "Economic Analysis of International Law," at 25.

negotiate with all other UNCLOS parties. Even if there are now 150 UNCLOS parties,[24] such negotiations remain, in principle, feasible as compared to negotiating with thousands of potential victims every time you drive your car.

At the same time, other elements can make transaction costs in international negotiations much higher than in domestic law. As opposed to negotiations between individuals or unitary actors, negotiations between states are likely to be complex and time consuming. As Putnam pointed out, state-to-state negotiations are two-level games.[25] At a first level of domestic politics, domestic constituencies and stakeholders must first formulate a position. At a second level of international politics, states must then agree amongst themselves. As these two levels constantly interact – international negotiators may have to report back or ask authority from, for example, parliament – arriving at an agreed text takes time, energy and considerable expense. Even if the creation of multilateral institutions (such as the UN in New York, WTO in Geneva or UNESCO in Paris) may have replaced dispersed bilateral negotiations with more uniform negotiations in the same context and city, other developments may have neutralized these savings. First, most of the large multilateral organizations make decisions only by consensus. As a result, agreement is needed not just on a bilateral level but as between, for example, 150 players in the UNCLOS or the WTO.

[24] See the Status of UNCLOS Ratification at www.un.org/Depts/los/reference_files/status2006.pdf (last visited 17 September 2007).

[25] Robert D. Putnam, "Diplomacy and Domestic Politics: The Logic of Two-Level Games" (1988), 42 *IO* 427, at 434.

Second, the rise of representative democracy both domestically and at the international level has considerably expanded the number of stakeholders in international negotiations (be it federal and sub-federal legislators, individuals, NGOs, companies, professional organizations or other international organizations), thereby increasing overall transaction costs. On balance, one can therefore expect that Calabresi and Melamed's third reason for liability rules (high transaction costs) can find particular application in the international context.

4 Arguments for a lower level of protection in international law

The discussion so far has centered on the arguments and criteria used by Calabresi and Melamed in the domestic law context. This book has made the case that, in international law as well, entitlements ought to be protected by a default property rule, for reasons of contractual freedom and welfare maximization and, an element specific to international law, because property protection requires the least amount of intervention. Similarly, the Calabresi and Melamed arguments for deviation to either inalienability or liability protection were found to be largely applicable also to international law, with the exception of free-load (as the consent rule in international law makes it difficult to impose a liability rule on free-riding states against their will). In this section and the next, criteria other than those addressed by Calabresi and Melamed are pointed at as arguments that may, or should, in the mind of treaty negotiators tip the balance either in favor of a *lower* level of protection (be it liability protection, or property protection instead of inalienability) or a *higher* level of protection (be it inalienability, or property protection instead of liability protection). The chapter concludes with an overall matrix where both the default rule and the reasons or criteria that may warrant deviation from that rule are summarized in a single table.

(a) The need for flexibility to attract participation and prevent exit

A first argument that militates for weaker protection of international law and against, in particular, inalienability relates to the largely consensual nature of international law-making. Fixing entitlements as inalienable can make it harder for states to join the norm or treaty regime in the first place: if a state knows that the new rule will be binding on it without the possibility for subsequent contracting out, it will think twice before signing on. Inalienability can, in this sense, exacerbate the problem of attracting participation. Even states that did contract into a regime of inalienability may, when found to be in violation, opt for leaving the regime altogether rather than strictly complying with it (the risk of exit that comes with inalienability).

International labor standards created under the auspices of the International Labor Organization (ILO) offer a good example of how treaties must balance universality and flexibility. To be effective, ILO standards should ideally be applied on a universal basis, that is, in all countries. Yet, to achieve universality, that is, to attract participation by all countries, ILO standards must offer flexibility to allow for the diverse cultural and historical backgrounds, legal systems and levels of economic development of ILO members.[26] A similar trade-off between universality and inalienability, on the one hand, and flexibility to attract participation, on the other, can be found in the *Reservations to the Convention on Genocide* case.[27] In that case, the International Court of Justice (ICJ) had to decide whether or not reservations to the 1948 Convention on the Prevention and Punishment of the Crime of Genocide were permissible. A negative answer would have strengthened the convention as such and confirmed its inalienable features; a positive answer would have offered flexibility which, in turn, could attract more states into signing the convention in the first place. The ICJ leaned toward the latter option, deciding that, even if some parties to the convention objected to a reservation, the reserving state "can be regarded as being a party to the Convention if the reservation is compatible with the object and purpose of the Convention."[28] Article 19 of the 1969 Vienna Convention on the Law of Treaties incorporates this principle.

(b) The consent rule as well as uncertainty may require incomplete contracting and flexibility

A second feature that may favor a lower level of protection for specific international law entitlements is the

[26] International Labour Office, *Rules of the Game: A Brief Introduction to International Labour Standards* (Geneva: ILO Publications, 2005), at 16.

[27] *Reservations to the Convention on Genocide, ICJ Rep* 1951, 15.

[28] *Ibid.*, at 21, 24.

problems related to the consent rule and general uncertainty as to the future. Especially when multilaterally negotiated with high numbers of states, the requirement of consent by each and every player often leads to a common lowest denominator of vague rules and constructive ambiguity. To prevent renegotiation or further refinement of such "incomplete contracts," that is, to make such entitlements inalienable, is then hardly an optimal solution. This explains why many of today's core multilateral treaties – such as the UN Convention on the Law of the Sea or the Convention on Biological Diversity – are in many ways relatively broad framework agreements that permit further specification in regional or bilateral agreements.[29]

International norms are, moreover, prone to be incomplete contracts on more standard grounds of general uncertainty as to the future.[30] When states draft treaties, especially in complex and evolving fields such as trade or environmental protection, negotiators are unlikely to discuss and fix rules for each and every situation that may arise in the future. Doing so would be too time-consuming and difficult (that is, involve transaction costs that are too high).

[29] See Article 311 of UNCLOS. For a discussion see Rudiger Wolfrum and Nele Matz, *Conflicts in International Environmental Law* (Berlin: Springer, 2003).

[30] See George Downs and David Rocke, *Optimal Imperfection: Domestic Uncertainty and Institutions in International Relations* (Princeton: Princeton University Press, 1995); Warren Schwartz and Alan Sykes, "The Economic Structure of Renegotiation and Dispute Resolution in the World Trade Organization" (2002), 31 *J Leg Stud* 179; and Henrik Horn, Giovanni Maggi and Robert W. Staiger, "The GATT/WTO as an Incomplete Contract," mimeo, 2006 (available at www.econ-law.se/HMS-5April2006.pdf, last visited 17 September 2007).

Moreover, even if negotiators were willing to pay these costs, it is humanly impossible to foresee the future: international conditions may change (be it the world economy, political alliances or natural disasters) and domestically as well, politicians are replaced and the preferences of their constituencies may alter. As Sykes pointed out, "[t]reaties are often negotiated under conditions of uncertainty. A variety of shocks may cause particular commitments to become inefficient, or may leave some signatory worse off than it would be by exiting."[31] Similarly, Rosendorff and Milner demonstrated that flexibility or what they call escape clauses – which, in effect, are liability rules where entitlements can be taken unilaterally, albeit often on a temporary basis, subject to compensation – are "an efficient equilibrium under conditions of domestic uncertainty."[32] More generally, "the greater the uncertainty that political leaders face about their ability to maintain domestic compliance with international agreements in the future, the more likely agreements are to contain escape clauses."[33] Crucially, and confirming that harder law is not always better law, incorporating flexibility, escape clauses or liability protection in circumstances of high uncertainty does not necessarily undermine the effectiveness of the treaty. On the contrary, as Rosendorff and Milner put it, "[i]nternational institutions that include an escape clause

[31] Alan Sykes, "The Economics of Public International Law," John M. Olin Law and Economics Working Paper No. 216, July 2004, at 16.

[32] B. Peter Rosendorff and Helen Milner, "The Optimal Design of International Trade Institutions: Uncertainty and Escape" (2001), 55 IO 829, at 831.

[33] *Ibid.*

generate more durable and stable cooperative international regimes, and are easier to achieve ex ante."[34]

For all these reasons, state-negotiated norms, even more so than contracts between private operators, are likely to be incomplete contracts that require a degree of flexibility. To protect entitlements thus allocated as inalienable may then not be optimal. Indeed, when faced with high levels of uncertainty, treaty negotiators may, if other prerequisites are met, be advised to protect entitlements through a mere liability rule. The treaty may then provide that a party can unilaterally take entitlements or defect at a price – i.e., whenever, for some reason or another, the cost of performance exceeds the damage caused by defection. If this price is set correctly, and the system can ensure that any victims are effectively made whole (the "other prerequisites" referred to in the previous sentence and further discussed below), liability protection can then facilitate efficient transfers and with it overall welfare. Or to use the terminology of escape clauses rather than liability protection, treaty design can be optimal if negotiators "choose a cost so that escape clauses are neither too cheap to use (encouraging frequent recourse, effectively reducing the benefits of cooperation) nor too expensive (such that they are rarely used leading to an increased chance of systemic breakdown)."[35] In contrast, in other situations where domestic uncertainty is less persuasive and consequential, like arms control (where the public and interest groups tend to be less organized and involved as compared to, for example, trade), liability protection or escape clauses are less appropriate. The ABM treaty, most of the

[34] *Ibid.*, at 829. [35] *Ibid.*, at 829.

SALT treaties and the INF treaties, for example, do not contain liability protection or escape mechanisms that allow temporary abrogation of the agreements.[36]

(c) Legitimacy concerns

A third potential argument against too high a level of protection for international law relates to the degree of legitimacy of international law itself. So far, this book has taken the legitimacy of international law for granted. For example, we have presumed that – through the consent rule – international entitlements are allocated in a transparent and equitable way. In a domestic legal system where democratically elected lawmakers allocate and shift entitlements this presumption is strong. In international law, however, the legitimacy of norms is sometimes questioned.

First, legitimacy concerns have been raised because of who creates custom and negotiates treaties, namely predominantly the executive branch of government to the detriment of national parliaments, and very often including also state representatives who are not democratically responsible yet may have a definite influence on how international law is made and enforced.[37] Secondly, the legitimacy of

[36] *Ibid.*, at 830.

[37] See, for example, J. H. H. Weiler and Iulia Motoc, "Taking Democracy Seriously: The Normative Challenges to the International Legal System," in Stefan Griller (ed.), *International Economic Governance and Non-Economic Concerns* (European Community Studies Association of Austria Publication Series 5 2003), 67 ("You take the obedience claim of international law and couple it with the conflation

international law has been questioned because of how difficult it is to change or adapt international law to new circumstances: once negotiated, signed and ratified, the consent rule and rules on the modification of custom make it extremely difficult to optimally adjust the allocation of international entitlements.[38] Thirdly, critics have doubted the legitimacy of certain international norms on the ground that weak states have, for economic, political or other reasons, little choice but to join a treaty or treaty amendment making their formal

of government and State which international law posits and you get nothing more than a monstrous empowerment of the executive branch at the expense of other political estates"); Curtis Bradley, "International Delegations, the Structural Constitution, and Non-Self-Execution" (2002), 55 *Stanford LR* 1,571, at 1,558 ("transfers of authority by the United States to international institutions could be said to raise 'delegation concerns.' These concerns relate to democratic accountability, shifts in the balance of power between the federal branches, and erosion of the U.S. system of federalism"); and Eyal Benvenisti, "Exit and Voice in the Age of Globalization" (1999), 98 *Michigan LR* 167, at 200 (arguing that ratification cannot cure the democratic difficulties in the treaty-making process).

38 See, for example, Jed Rubenfeld, "Unilateralism and Constitutionalism" (2004), 79 *NYULR* 1,971, at 2,007 ("Treaties are exceptions to ordinary lawmaking. Not only are they made outside the ordinary, democratic lawmaking process, but they can also claim to impose obligations on a country that the nation's legislature cannot thereafter amend or undo") and Jacob Cogan, "Noncompliance and the International Rule of Law" (2006), 31 *Yale J Int L* 189, at 197 (advocating what he calls operational noncompliance "in cases in which time is a factor or in situations in which consensus (as to reinterpretation or renegotiation) is unachievable – that is, in situations in which the international legal system, because of its decentralized lawmaking process, cannot accommodate current or developing conceptions of lawfulness").

consent an insufficient basis for those states to be legitimately held against the norms in question.[39]

This is not the place to evaluate whether or not there is a legitimacy deficit in international law. If at all present, this deficit would, in any event, vary across international norms and between states. What matters for present purposes is that where such deficit exists, it may offer an additional reason to think twice before protecting entitlements as inalienable.[40] In some cases, it may even tip the balance in favor of liability protection, where states are permitted to take entitlements for as long as they pay compensation for them. In those circumstances, liability protection could, in other words, offer a democratic safety-valve: if, based on new circumstances or changed preferences, a population changes its mind and democratically opposes a treaty obligation, under a liability rule, this opposition can be given effect, yet without harming others as liability protection implies full compensation of all victims. Similarly, for those who believe that current international law is lopsided in favor of economic globalization and lags behind in environmental and

[39] See Joseph Weiler, "The Geology of International Law – Governance, Democracy and Legitimacy" (2004), 64 *ZaöRV* 547, at 557 ("Increasingly international regimes ... are negotiated on a take-it-or-leave-it basis ... But for most States both the Take it is fictitious and the Leave it is even more. The consent given by these 'sovereign' states is not much different to the 'consent' that each of us gives, when we upgrade the operating system of our computer and blithely click the 'I Agree' button on the Microsoft Terms and Conditions").

[40] Some may go as far as using Marxist-type arguments against international law as a law that protects the strong and the status quo and hence ought not to be made inalienable.

social globalization,[41] liability protection can offer an interesting tool. To avoid an even bigger divide, one could then argue that, for example, trade and investment agreements should only be protected by a liability rule. On this view, only once stronger rules materialize in the non-economic sector should stronger protection of trade and investment entitlements follow.

5 Arguments for a higher level of protection in international law

Given earlier arguments in favor of weaker protection of international law, what stops international negotiators from setting up liability regimes? In other words, why prevent the apparently efficient and politically desirable outcome of the take-and-pay principle? More specifically, if a state takes another state's entitlement, fully compensates the victim and still gains, overall welfare increases at no one's expense: the violator is better off without any loss to the victim. So why should we ever set up property rules that categorically prevent such unilateral takings? Put differently, what is wrong with American voluntarism and its preference for liability rules and efficient breach?

As noted earlier, in domestic law, the core objection to liability rules is contractual freedom: if the entitlement

[41] See Gary Gereffi and Frederick Mayer, "Making Globalization Work," February 2004 (paper on file with author) at 2, who refer to a "partially globalized world" and find a "global governance deficit of considerable magnitude."

does not change hands freely between a willing seller and a willing buyer, we must presume that such exchange does not increase welfare (i.e., the buyer does not value the entitlement more than the seller). As each individual or state is, in principle, in the best position to appreciate its preferences and to determine, for itself, the value it gives to entitlements, only where the market fails (i.e., when faced with strategic behavior or high transaction costs) should we force exchange, i.e., permit unilateral takings under a liability rule.[42]

There are, however, crucially important additional caveats against liability protection, some of which are specific to international law:

1 where international law does not offer third-party dispute settlement, the collective valuation central to liability protection is simply unavailable;
2 even where there is collective valuation, it can be costly and prone to errors;
3 international entitlements often involve unique goods that are difficult to price;
4 stability and the need to make credible commitments are vital in international affairs;
5 there are inequalities between states.

[42] As Eric Posner points out, "the simplest defense of specific performance [i.e., protecting contracts with a property rule] is that if parties are rational, they will design an optimal contract and courts should enforce their terms rather than giving the parties an option (expectation damages) when they did not bargain for it": Eric Posner, "Economic Analysis of Contract Law after Three Decades: Success or Failure" (2002), University of Chicago Law and Economics, Olin Working Paper No. 146, available at http://ssrn.com/abstract=304977, at 7, note 13, last visited 17 September 2007.

Finally, although these two objections can be made against the broader law and economics model of this book as a whole (including the default rule of property protection), this is a good place to elaborate on two critiques mentioned earlier, namely:

6 states may not internalize costs or maximize internal welfare;
7 states are not unitary actors, meaning that both taking and selling international entitlements can leave individuals or companies within states worse off.

All seven of these arguments can also be seen as reasons why American voluntarism (which favors the protection of international law entitlements through a simple liability rule) risks in many cases, and in the current context of international law, being a step too far.

(a) Absence of collective valuation

As noted earlier, liability protection necessitates higher levels of intervention than property protection. Somewhat ironically, therefore, when American voluntarists or other critics of international law argue in favor of efficient breach or liability protection, they advocate the creation of more (not fewer) international institutions and more (not less) central intervention in what is otherwise the free market of entitlements. Put differently, although advocates of American voluntarism, liability protection and efficient breach often come from politically conservative circles, in effect what they argue for goes against free market ideas and liberal capitalism. They must, in other words, be careful what they wish for.

As Dunoff and Trachtman point out, under liability rules "courts set the price of transfer, and the 'owner' may be forced to accept the price so set. Thus, the choice between property and liability is a partial choice between the market [property] and the state [liability] as the institution for effecting transfers of relevant assets."[43] Although entitlements protected by a liability rule can be unilaterally taken (thereby limiting the amount of intervention required to protect them), once taken, the value of those entitlements must be objectively valuated by a third party. This neutral *ex post* valuation to force an efficient exchange is a type and degree of intervention not required under a property regime. Under a property rule the valuation of entitlements is left to the parties themselves. A crucial requirement for liability protection is, therefore, the availability of a collective valuation mechanism.

Given the absence of centralized enforcement in international law – there is no international court or tribunal that states can automatically resort to for compensation in case their entitlements are taken – liability protection will in many cases be out of the question. Without a collective valuation system, liability protection risks, indeed, amounting to the law of the jungle: yes, states could then take entitlements only if they pay for them, but without a court to set the value of the compensation, liability protection may

[43] Dunoff and Trachtman, "Economic Analysis of International Law," at 25.

well offer no protection at all. This also explains why, somewhat counterintuitively, one expects the lower degree of liability protection in those regimes of international law that are most developed and institutionalized, that is, which benefit from a strong dispute settlement mechanism and efficient back-up enforcement able to set and collect compensation. Put differently, the lower level of liability protection requires higher levels of international regulation.

(b) The cost and possible errors of collective valuation

Even where international law does provide a mechanism for collective valuation, the cost and possible errors of collective valuation can provide powerful arguments against liability protection. Two types of costs can be distinguished:[44] first, the cost of setting up and running a court system that objectively values entitlements; second, the errors made by such a court system in assessing the true value of an entitlement to its holder.

Obviously, as in domestic law, setting up and running an international court or tribunal costs money: headquarters must be found and maintained; judges, staff and interpreters need to be appointed and paid; and the disputing parties themselves spend time and resources preparing and pleading their case. More importantly, however, in the international

[44] See Daniel Friedman, "The Efficient Breach Fallacy" (1989), 18 *J Leg Stud* 1, at 6–7, and Alan Schwartz, "The Case for Specific Performance" (1979), 89 *Yale LJ* 271.

context, are possible errors of valuation by international courts or tribunals. Such errors risk that liability protection does not maximize welfare: *under*-compensation does not fully compensate the victim, thereby making the transfer Pareto undesirable and potentially overall inefficient; *over*-compensation pays the victim more than she is harmed and is said to deter efficient breach.[45]

The risk of under-compensation is generally considered as most important. As Richard Craswell points out in the context of US law, "expectation damages as awarded in law often fall short of a truly compensatory measure due to the exclusion of such items as attorneys' fees, immeasurable subjective losses and 'unforeseeable damages'. Other rules excuse defendants from liability of expectation damages in cases of mistake or impracticability, or when clauses limiting the defendant's liability are upheld."[46] The limited evidence available in the international context confirms this tendency to under-value harm or compensation.[47] This is the case, for example, in arbitrations tasked to set the permissible level of

[45] Eric Posner, for example, has taken the view that "expectation damages are . . . undesirable if courts have trouble determining the parties' valuations at the time of breach. The better remedy is specific performance, because the latter does not require the court to determine the promisee's valuation": Posner, "Economic Analysis of Contract Law after Three Decades," at 7.

[46] Richard Craswell, "Contract Remedies, Renegotiation and the Theory of Efficient Breach" (1987), 61 *Southern California LR* 629, at 637.

[47] See Petros Mavroidis, "Remedies in the WTO Legal System: Between a Rock and a Hard Place" (2000), 11 *EJIL* 763, at 769 (referring to "the fallacy of full recovery" and stating that "courts normally have a tendency to downplay requested damages").

trade retaliation in response to WTO breach.[48] The same conservative valuations are witnessed in investor–state arbitrations and before the International Court of Justice.[49]

48 In WTO arbitrations that determine the level of trade suspension which is "equivalent to the level of nullification or impairment" caused by WTO breach (Understanding on Rules and Procedures Governing the Settlement of Disputes, 15 April 1994, entry into force 1 January 1995, 1869 UNTS 401(DSU), Article 22.4), awards have, indeed, been rather conservative. In *US–Bananas*, arbitrators refused to count US fertilizer and machinery exports to Latin America as well as US capital, management and packaging services offered in respect of Latin American banana exports to the EC (arguing that it was for those Latin American countries to claim these harms). In *EC – Hormones*, the arbitrators noted: "we need to guard against claims of lost opportunities where the causal link with the inconsistent hormone ban is less than apparent" (para. 41) and rejected harm with "too remote" or "too speculative" a causal link (para. 77). In *US–1916 Act*, the arbitrators insisted on "credible, factual, and verifiable information" (para. 5.54) and stressed that "this prudent approach ... is appropriate" (para. 5.57). As a result, they rejected to count any settlement under the 1916 Act that was not disclosed (para. 5.63). Since under US law most (if not all) settlements are bound by confidentiality rules, no settlements are currently covered. The same arbitrators refused to count the "chilling effect" of merely having legislation in place (even if it is not actually applied) for being "too speculative, and too remote" (para. 5.69), noting dryly that "a quantification of the chilling effect is not possible" (para. 5.72). While accepting final damages amounts and fines in judgments under the 1916 Act, the arbitrators also refused to count litigation costs (para. 5.76).

49 See, for example, Serge Lazareff, "Assessing Damages – Are Arbitrators Good at It? Should They Be Assisted by Experts? Should They Be Entitled To Decide *ex aequo et bono*? – Some War Stories" (2005), 6 *J World Investment Trade* 17: "Assessing damages is the *parent pauvre* of arbitration, the neglected aspect. It is almost, in the context of arbitration, the midnight clause of a contract, and it is very distressing

This tendency to put conservative estimates on harm is probably inspired by a high degree of deference by international courts to the sovereignty of states. Where the tribunal already intruded on this sovereignty by finding a violation, it is often naturally inclined to somewhat make up for this intrusion by low-balling the compensation to be paid for the violation.[50] In the context of international environmental law as well, more specifically oil pollution at sea, it has been pointed out that actual compensation is systematically lower than the harm suffered.[51]

to read in so many awards that '*the Tribunal, having at its disposal all the elements of the case, orders A to pay B US$140 million*'; finished" and Debra Steger, "Dispute Settlement under the NAFTA," 2006 manuscript, available with author, at 8 ("the tribunals established [under NAFTA chapter 11] to date (with two or three notable exceptions) have been relatively conservative in their findings and awards of damages."

50 An interesting provision in an earlier draft of the 2001 ILC Articles on State Responsibility provided the following limitation on a state's obligation of reparation: "In no case shall reparation result in depriving the population of a State of its own means of subsistence": Article 42.3 of the Draft Articles on State Responsibility (1996), Text of the Draft Articles Provisionally adopted by the Commission on first reading, UN Doc A/51/10, Report of the International Law Commission on the Work of its 48th Session, 58. This limitation, which would, of course, only have enhanced the scope for under-compensation, was not withheld in the final 2001 ILC Articles.

51 See Volkmar J. Hartje, "Oil Pollution by Tanker Accidents: Liability versus Regulation" (1984), 24 *Nat Res J* 41, at 44 (pointing at high transaction costs for victims to actually recover damages, e.g., because they may face different courts with overlapping jurisdictions or because they may have suffered minor harm and class actions are not permitted).

Thus, where treaty negotiators do consider the inclusion of liability rules, it is important not only to set up a dispute settlement system to award compensation; such a system must also ensure that the level of compensation is accurately calculated. If compensation is systematically too low, any reference to "efficient breach" becomes a mockery as the forced exchange is then not "efficient," at least not in Pareto terms: even if the exchange were to increase overall welfare (the net cost of compliance is higher than the net cost of defection), it makes one of the parties worse off, namely the victim who is not fully compensated.

(c) International entitlements as unique goods

Correct valuation of an entitlement becomes even more difficult if the entitlement has subjective value to its holder. Non-compensation of this subjective value may well be what prevented the consensual transfer of the entitlement in the first place. In international law this problem of so-called "unique goods" and non-monetized exchange can be particularly acute. As pointed out earlier, transactions in international affairs revolve around a market for power. This market is, as Dunoff and Trachtman observed, "not normally a cash market. Rather, it is most often a barter market, with all the difficulties and transaction costs of barter."[52]

[52] Dunoff and Trachtman, "Economic Analysis of International Law," at 19. In support, see Schwartz and Sykes, "The Economic Structure of Renegotiation and Dispute Resolution in the WTO," at 187 ("the harm done to political officials by a breach of promise in the WTO is no

As opposed to fungible goods (such as money, wheat or cars) which are commonly traded, many international law entitlements involve unique goods which are not often traded and have high levels of subjective value, making third-party valuation extremely difficult.[53] How should we value and price, for example, intrusion in a country's airspace? What is the value of a country's agricultural exports if agriculture is said to fulfill not only economic but also environmental, life-style and social functions? What is the value of cultural identity, GMO-free supermarkets or a pristine environment in a poor developed country as opposed to a rich country?[54] Given the enormous economic, social and cultural diversity between states, the value of a particular entitlement is likely to vary

doubt difficult to measure precisely, and when damages are hard to calculate, that fact is usually thought to be a heavy thumb on the scale of favoring a property rule over a liability rule").

[53] Kronman argues that the common law efficiently reserves specific performance for disputes involving valuation problems such as those involving unique goods: Anthony Kronman, "Specific Performance" (1978), 45 *U Chicago LR* 351.

[54] In this context, Jide Nzelibe argues that continued uncertainty as to a country's costs of breach and retaliation may actually contribute to compliance. He uses uncertainty as an argument against efficient breach or liability protection: "the efficient breach approach seems inappropriate when applied to the WTO context because it can eliminate or substantially undermine the uncertainty that is inherent in trade disputes and negotiations, rendering retaliation ineffective as an enforcement mechanism . . . uncertainty about each state's retaliation costs increases the chance that retaliation will be an effective deterrent": Jide Nzelibe, "The Credibility Imperative: The Political Dynamics of Retaliation in the WTO's Dispute Resolution Mechanism" (2005), 6 *Theoretical Inquiries in Law* 215, at 244.

widely between states. Any attempt at collective valuation, in particular when such is done exclusively by foreign judges, may therefore include serious errors of under- or over-valuation.[55]

(d) Stability and the need to make credible commitments

Another argument against liability protection closely linked to contractual freedom and the consensual exchange of entitlements mentioned earlier, is: stability. One need not even agree with David Hume that stability of possession is one of the dominant rules of society[56] or that breach of contract (even when compensated) violates Aristotelian virtues of promise-keeping and justice,[57] to appreciate that liability rules may affect the security of transactions and

[55] The first and core hypothesis in the positive model of optimal international law enforcement of Professors Scott and Stephan – whose main distinction is between formal and informal enforcement – makes a similar point related to valuation or verifiability: "States and other actors will rely on informal mechanisms for international law enforcement whenever applying the rules requires information that cannot be verified by an independent observer except at a high cost and where effective and verifiable proxies for that information are not readily available to an independent observer": Robert Scott and Paul Stephan, *The Limits of Leviathan* (Cambridge: Cambridge University Press, 2006), at 255.

[56] David Hume, *A Treatise of Human Nature*, 2nd edn, ed. L. A. Selby-Bigge (Oxford: Oxford University Press, 1978 [1739–40]), at 484–516.

[57] James Gordley, *The Philosophical Origins of Modern Contract Law* (New York: Oxford University Press, 1991), at 11, 112. Or as Charles Fried put it succinctly: a "contract must be kept because a promise must be

societal stability at large.[58] Even if full compensation follows, the unilateral taking of entitlements disrupts the grievant's world.[59] In contracts with multiple parties, such as multilateral treaties, it may upset a large number of parties and even incite third parties to engage in reciprocal breach (the risk of emulation).[60]

Lest it be forgotten, secure property rights are one of the fundamental tenets of free market economies. It is the assurance of property protection that drives owners to use their assets to profit themselves, and with it society at large. A constant threat of confiscation under a liability rule, albeit with full compensation, is no incentive to invest in or develop one's assets. As Alan Greenspan – hardly a European absolutist – put it in his recent biography, "[k]nowing that the government will protect one's property encourages

kept": Charles Fried, *Contract as Promise: A Theory of Contractual Obligation* (Cambridge, Mass.: Harvard University Press, 1981, at 17).

58 See, for an example, Fried, *Contract as Promise.*

59 As Coleman and Kraus put it: "It is surely odd to claim that an individual's right is protected when another individual is permitted to force a transfer at a price set by third parties. Isn't the very idea of a forced transfer contrary to the autonomy or liberty thought constitutive of rights?": Jules Coleman and Jody Kraus, "Rethinking the Theory of Legal Rights" (1986), 95 *Yale LJ* 1,335, at 1,338–9.

60 See, for example, Sungjoon Cho, "The Nature of Remedies in International Trade Law" (2004), 65 *U Pittsburgh LR* 763, at 808, explaining WTO remedies and the property rule inherent in it with reference to "growing norm-building that can ensure a stable and predictable operation of the system ... WTO remedies not only address disputes but also prevent them" and regarding "WTO remedies as public goods for all Members beyond a mere instrument that settles and satisfies particular parties concerned in specific cases."

citizens to take business risks, a prerequisite of wealth creation and economic growth. Few will risk their capital if the rewards are going to be subject to arbitrary seizure by the government or mobsters."[61] The analogy to property protection of international entitlements and how it creates a stable system for welfare maximization between states is readily made.

Sociological studies have confirmed that people and businessmen highly value the principle that commitments are to be honored (sanctity of contract). Stewart Macaulay's famous study of relations among close-knit Wisconsin businessmen, for example, turned up two prominent contract norms. The first is that "commitments are to be honored in almost all situations."[62] To return to Alan Greenspan, in his

[61] Greenspan, "Age of Turbulence," at 140 and 251 ("It has been startling to see over the years what even a little private ownership will do. When China granted highly diluted rights of ownership to the rural residents ... yield per acre and rural standards of living rose measurably. It was an unrelenting embarrassing stain on the Soviet Union's central planning ... As living requires physical property – food, clothes, homes – people need the legal protection to own and dispose of such property without the threat of arbitrary confiscation by the state or mobs on the street").

[62] The second contract norm that Macaulay identified was that "one ought to produce a good product and stand behind it": Stewart Macaulay, "Non-Contractual Relations in Business" (1963), 28 *Am Soc R* 555. See also H. L. A. Hart, *The Concept of Law* (Oxford: Oxford University Press, 1961), at 192–3, identifying the rule requiring the keeping of promises as part of a minimum natural law of a society. It has also been argued that a disposition to honor commitments enhances a person's chances of survival: Robert Frank, "If *Homo*

view one of the core requirements for "the proper functioning of market capitalism" is "trust in the word of others":

> Where the rule of law prevails, despite everyone's right to legal redress of a perceived grievance [e.g., under a liability rule], if there is more than a small fraction of outstanding contracts that require adjudication, court systems would be overwhelmed, as would society's ability to be governed by the rule of law. This implies that in a free society ... the vast majority of transactions must be voluntary, which, of necessity, presupposes trust in the word of those with whom we do business – in almost all cases, strangers."[63]

More broadly, Paul Epstein has expressed the view that "[t]he choice between property rules and liability rules should normally be resolved in favor of the former to preserve the stability of possession and social expectations that are necessary for the growth of any complex social order."[64]

Closely related to the argument of stability, if transactions and the possession of entitlements are not secure (as risks being the case under liability protection) making credible commitments becomes more difficult. Yet, one of the core functions of international law and institutions, operating as they do without central enforcement, is to enable credible commitment.[65] To resolve international problems, in

Economicus Could Choose His Own Utility Function, Would He Want One with a Conscience?" (1987), 77 *Am Econ R* 593.

[63] Greenspan, "Age of Turbulence," at 256.

[64] Paul Epstein, "A Clear View of *The Cathedral*: The Dominance of Property Rules" (1996), 106 *Yale LJ* 2,091, at 2,120.

[65] See Andrew Guzman, "International Law: A Compliance Based Theory" (2002), 90 *California LR* 1,823; Andrew Guzman, "Reputation

particular to transcend so-called prisoners' dilemmas and collective action situations, states will only commit themselves and cooperate if other states do the same and make their commitments credible. A commitment protected only by the take-and-pay principle of a liability rule may not be credible enough. As a result, no deal may be made, fewer states may participate or fewer commitments may be entered into.

As interactions between states are repeat games on a variety of topics, frequent unilateral buy-outs by a state, even if compensated, can also make future commitments of that state (in the same or in a different context) less credible. With past experiences of buy-outs, why would you believe this time that a government will keep its promise? Faced with commitments that are not credible enough, states, like individuals in private contracts, may be able to secure future performance by means of clumsy security devices such as bonds and hostages, but only at the expense of high transaction costs.[66]

Moreover, recall that international relations are two-level games. Hence, states sometimes make international law not only as a commitment against other states, but also as a commitment toward their own domestic constituencies.

and International Law" (2005), 34 *Georgia J Int Comp L* 379, and Kal Raustiala, "Refining the Limits of International Law" (2005), 34 *Georgia J Int Comp L* 423.

66 See Anthony T. Kronman, "Contract Law and the State of Nature" (1985), 1 *JL Econ Org* 5. Also Daniel Friedmann, "The Efficient Breach Fallacy" (1989), 18 *J Leg Stud* 1, at 7: "If a party in need of contracting with another cannot rely on the contract to guarantee performance, then he may turn to other more costly and less efficient means (for example, becoming a self-supplier or vertically integrating with his supplier) to gain greater assurance that he will get what he seeks."

One reason why countries commit, for example, to trade liberalization or human rights and international protections for minority groups is often to lock in domestic reform or to tie their hands, and the hands of future governments, to resist against present and future domestic pressure groups. If these pressure groups know that the commitment can simply be bought off, governments may not be able to resist. Liability protection, therefore, can threaten credible commitment as against both other states and domestic players. Put differently, the welfare gains of liability protection may be outweighed by welfare losses due to a lack of credible commitment either internationally or at home. When selecting the optimal level of protection in new treaties, negotiators must make this trade-off between flexibility and commitment, a balance that is likely to be different for each treaty, as well as for each country considering the adoption of a new treaty.

(e) Inequalities between states

A further element to keep in mind when considering liability rules for international law is the huge inequalities between states. States such as the United States are immeasurably richer and politically more powerful than states such as Burkina Faso or Bangladesh. In domestic contract law terms, a treaty between the United States and Bangladesh is like a contract between Microsoft and an individual living below the poverty line. Liability protection in this context of huge inequalities creates the risk that the take-and-pay principle works only for the rich and powerful. Liability rules in the WTO context, for example, could grant the EC and the United

States a democratic safety valve and permit them to breach and pay their way out if welfare maximization so directs. Poor developing countries, in contrast, may not always have this option, either because they cannot pay for their takings or breach, or because a taking or breach risks the trigger of hidden reprisals. The same could happen to smaller developed countries. Where the United States may not easily be stopped from discriminating or expropriating foreign investments, notwithstanding the NAFTA obligation to pay compensation for it, the chilling effect on Canada (either through the US government or through the pressure of foreign investors more generally) may be substantial and prevent Canada from action even where it would maximize welfare. Now, if the poor or relatively weak cannot, or dare not, take entitlements even where it would maximize welfare, welfare losses occur and it is hard to speak of a truly operational, let alone equitable, liability rule.

From a victim's perspective as well, liability protection or an offer of compensation or retaliation may not work if one is weak or poor. In the WTO context, for example, remedy for breach takes the form not of monetary compensation but of a right to impose compensatory trade restrictions. Now, if one is a poor developing country, victim of WTO breach, one may not even have enough trade with the violating WTO member to actually be able to exercise the retaliation rights obtained.[67] If so, breach cannot technically

[67] In *Canada – Aircraft Credits and Guarantees*, for example, the relatively small size of the Brazilian market actually worked against Brazil as a complainant. It was used as an argument to *lower* Brazil's rights to trade

be set off or rebalanced and any reference to efficient breach is wholly inappropriate.

Finally, rather than worry about not enough "efficient breach" by poor states, an opposing argument exists that may raise fears that poor states will too easily defect under a liability rule. Indeed, when potential defectors are too poor, there is a risk of non-payment and the take-and-pay principle of the liability rule is in danger. In other words, certain states may simply be so poor that they do not have the money or other resources to pay for their breach. This can lead to breach by poor countries without compensation and, therefore, welfare losses. On that ground, Richard Posner, for example, has argued that compensation was not a feasible alternative to retaliatory sanctions in early legal systems: with their very limited wealth, wrongdoers simply could not compensate their victims.[68] In international law, this risk of non-compensation and, with it, too many

retaliation. The arbitrators looked at the overall level of trade between Canada and Brazil (Canada's exports to Brazil were, according to Canada, US$591 million; according to Brazil, US$927 million) and found as follows (para. 3.42): "This disparity between the level of the proposed countermeasures [US$3.36 billion] and the total value of Brazil's imports of goods from Canada [between 0.5 and 1 US$ billion] is so large that, in our view, it is not fitting by way of response to the case at hand." The arbitrators finally awarded a little under US$250 million. Hence, instead of feeling pity for Brazil (and its low levels of imports from Canada), the arbitrators used this factor against Brazil. This is like saying that since the victim of a crime is poor or does not have the strength to retaliate, we must reduce the penalty on the wrongdoer.

68 Richard Posner, "A Theory of Primitive Society, with Special Reference to Law" (1980), 23 *JL Econ* 1.

defections by poor countries is mitigated by the fact, discussed in chapter 6, that it is mainly elements other than formal sanctions that induce compliance. These other elements (ranging from hidden reprisals and reciprocity to reputation and other community costs) will in most cases be enough to stop poor countries from breach, even where breach would not lead to recoverable compensation.

(f) States may not internalize costs or maximize welfare

This brings us to two core objections that can be raised against this book's broader law and economics or states-as-rational-actors model, mentioned earlier in chapter 3: first, states may not be rational utility-maximizers in the first place; second, states are not unitary actors. This section elaborates on the first objection; the next, on the second objection.

Unlike individuals or firms, states do not necessarily internalize all of the costs imposed on them.[69] To begin with, and quite obviously, politicians and bureaucrats making decisions on behalf of the state do not individually bear the costs of those decisions. When the US Congress decides to invade a country or the US President decides to impose safeguard duties on imported steel, the individual decision-makers

[69] See Eric Posner and Alan Sykes, "An Economic Analysis of State and Individual Responsibility under International Law," February 2006, at 13, available at http://papers.ssrn.com/sol3/papers.cfm?abstract_id=885197, last visited 17 September 2007.

do not pay the bill. Granted, the same is true when managers or board members make decisions on behalf of a firm. Yet, whereas firms are generally assumed to be profit maximizers and will therefore in principle internalize the costs imposed on them, states fulfill functions other than profit-maximization such as providing public goods, upholding certain values or increasing geopolitical power. States do not respond to shareholders with profit in mind, they respond to voters with a range of financial and other preferences. As a result, states may not react to monetary incentives, including those at work under a liability rule, the way firms do.[70] Consequently, one state may take another state's entitlement even if it puts the first state in a financially *worse* position (the compensation to be paid for the

[70] See Daryl J. Levinson, "Making Governments Pay: Markets, Politics and the Allocation of Constitutional Costs" (2000), 67 *Chicago LR* 345 (arguing that government officials may not regard the payment of a money judgment, which presents budgetary issues, with quite the same perspective as a private person who experiences possession and ownership more directly). In the context of making governments pay for expropriation or takings, see Lawrence Blume and Daniel L. Rubinfeld, "Compensation for Takings: An Economic Analysis" (1984), 72 *California LR* 569, and Vicki Been and Joel C. Beauvais, "The Global Fifth Amendment? NAFTA's Investment Protections and the Misguided Quest for an International 'Regulatory Takings' Doctrine" (2003), 78 *NYULR* 30 (arguing that government actors who decide on what property to use for public purposes do not bear the costs of that decision, or receive the benefits). In contrast, see Richard Epstein, *Takings: Private Property and the Power of Eminent Domain* (Cambridge, Mass.: Harvard University Press, 1985) (arguing that the requirement of just compensation will force government to internalize the costs of taking private property and tend to ensure that it is not taken unless its value in government hands is higher).

entitlement exceeds the economic benefit of having the entitlement). Of course, if the taker-state thereby expresses the net preferences of its people the outcome (though financially costly) continues to maximize welfare, as welfare is not a purely financial question of cost and benefit, but the aggregate of an individual's, a population's or a state's preferences. If, for example, the US people values the liberation of a suppressed people more than it costs the US to liberate that people, US intervention can be said to maximize US welfare. If it does not, US decision-makers risk losing the next election.

At the same time, however, public choice theory demonstrates that states, including democratic ones, do *not* always act in the aggregate interest of the population, even if such interests are broadly defined beyond mere financial cost-benefits.[71] In democratic states, public officials stand or fall not on the basis of the bottom line of the country's budget, but as a result of political elections. Hence, they can be captured by special interests and make decisions that favor those interests but harm the country's overall welfare. Most trade restrictions, for example, amount to shooting oneself in the foot (consumer prices increase more than any increase in producer surplus). Yet, states commonly restrict

[71] Robert Hudec goes a few steps further arguing that, in the context of WTO dispute settlement, governments "simply are not private litigants; they are governments – complex institutions known the world over for their inability to behave like rational beings": Robert Hudec, "Transcending the Ostensible: Some Reflections on the Nature of Litigation between Governments" (1987), 72 *Minnesota LR* 211.

trade so as to placate and confer special benefits to import competing companies. The situation in non-democratic states is worse: as dictators are not held accountable, their decisions – though likely maximizing the dictator's *individual* welfare – are not necessarily taken with the nation's overall welfare in mind.

If this is true – states (both democratic and dictatorial) act even if it reduces the overall welfare (broadly defined) of the country – the normative claim for liability rules and efficient breach is jeopardized. Liability rules and efficient breach are desirable only because they maximize welfare *without leaving anyone worse off*. They are, in other words, Pareto improving. When states do not internalize the compensation costs of taking entitlements or breaching obligations, that is, when they act even if it puts the country in an overall worse position, the transfer or breach is no longer Pareto superior and the *raison d'être* of liability rules and efficient breach evaporates. Iraq under Saddam Hussein may then invade Kuwait even if it harms overall Iraqi welfare. The United States may expropriate a Canadian investment even though the NAFTA compensation to be paid for it *outweighs* any US welfare gains. Equally, the European Union may then violate WTO rules even though the cost of retaliation is *higher* than the benefit of breach.

For dictators or elected officials who want to hold office such takings or transfers may be *politically* efficient. This explains why international negotiators may, as a descriptive matter, agree on liability rules or accept efficient breach regimes. Yet, as a normative matter, such transfers do not increase welfare (they are not Pareto improving) and are, therefore, not desirable in welfare terms. In the context of the GATT/WTO, for example, Warren Schwartz and Alan Sykes argue that the WTO is a system that promotes efficient breach in a political sense, for the political actors who negotiated the treaty. They refer to "joint political welfare maximization"[72] where "the metric of welfare for each signatory to a trade agreement will not be money, but instead will be the political welfare (votes, campaign contributions, or graft, as the case may be) of its political officials."[73] Based on this *political* analogy to efficient breach, they explain why WTO back-up enforcement is limited to compensation and equivalent retaliation: "When the political burden of performance to a promisor exceeds the political detriment of nonperformance to the promisee(s) ... nonperformance is jointly desirable."[74] Yet, Schwartz and Sykes never argue that breach of WTO rules combined with compensation or suffering equivalent retaliation maximizes inter-state welfare or is Pareto desirable in any economic sense. In other words, Schwartz and Sykes use a political analogy to efficient breach in order to *explain* what they regard as the current level of protection of WTO entitlements, not to advocate that this current level of protection is *normatively desirable* as welfare maximizing. In sum, their argument is that the WTO *is* a liability rule regime (an assessment I disagree with below), not that it *should* be one if the goal is to maximize welfare.

[72] Warren Schwartz and Alan Sykes, "The Economic Structure of Renegotiation and Dispute Resolution in the World Trade Organization" (2002), 31 *J Leg Stud* 179, at 180.

[73] *Ibid.*, at 184. [74] *Ibid.*

(g) States are not unitary actors

Piercing the state-to-state welfare maximization model even further, it is readily apparent that even where state conduct does maximize the population's aggregate welfare it may still create individual losers within the state. This is because states are not unitary actors. Focusing, first, on states *taking* entitlements, the taking with full compensation may well increase the state's overall welfare. Yet, quite often, it leaves some individuals within the state worse off. Although quite unlikely, the US imposition of a safeguard on steel imports may increase overall US welfare even if one counts for the cost of reciprocal trade retaliation against, say, US exports of oranges or textiles. The benefit to US steel producers could, somehow, outweigh the cost to US steel consumers (paying more for steel because of higher tariffs) combined with the cost to US oranges and textiles exporters (losing export markets due to the retaliation). Be this as it may, this constellation still reduces the individual welfare of both US steel consumers and US exporters of oranges and textiles. Unless the government were to redistribute some of the gains away from US steel producers (through, for example, cash payments or tax credits), from the perspective of US steel consumers and US exporters of oranges and textiles the transfer or breach is *not* maximizing welfare. Put differently, shift the unit of analysis from the state to individuals within the state and normatively speaking the transfer or breach is no longer Pareto superior (steel consumers and exporters of oranges and textiles lose) and, therefore, no longer desirable.

Moving, secondly, to states which *hold* entitlements and see those entitlements taken by another state with full compensation, the transfer or compensation may well leave overall welfare in the victim state intact. Yet, quite often, it leaves some individuals within that state worse off. Even if Kuwait were somehow fully compensated for an Iraqi invasion, there is no guarantee that the compensation trickles down to those individuals or companies within Kuwait who were actually harmed. Even if compensation were correctly valuated and fully paid (problems discussed above), the question of equitable redistribution within the state remains. Equally, trade compensation paid by the US for the imposition of a safeguard on EC steel may well keep overall EC welfare intact: the gain to EC exporters of, for example, cheese (if this is where the US opens its market as trade compensation) may neutralize the losses to EC steel exporters (who export less because of the safeguard). However, even if this were so, this constellation does not compensate individual EC exporters of steel. As the original complainants in the dispute, EC steel producers remain uncompensated: more exports of cheese do not wipe out their losses. Unless the EC were to redistribute some of the gains away from cheese exporters (through, for example, cash payments or tax credits), from the perspective of EC steel producers the transfer or breach is *not* maximizing welfare. Put differently, shift the unit of analysis from the state to individuals within the state and normatively speaking the transfer or breach is no longer Pareto superior (EC steel exporters lose), and therefore no longer desirable.

That states are not unitary actors and that international law entitlements do not uniformly operate in a state-to-state relationship is well illustrated when applying liability rules or efficient breach to entitlements under human rights conventions. Imagine states A and B, both bound by a human rights treaty against torture and gender discrimination. Both have, as a result, entitlements not to see the other engage in torture or gender discrimination. Imagine now that state A wants to torture some of its prisoners or sees a need to discriminate against women, and therefore decides to buy state B's entitlements to the contrary. To begin with, the decision by state A is unlikely to increase state A's overall welfare (confirming that states, in particular dictatorships, sometimes act against the aggregate welfare of their population). More importantly, even if the decision were somehow to increase overall welfare in state A, the torture or discrimination would surely leave individuals *within* state A worse off (those tortured or the women discriminated against). From their perspective, the transfer is *not* Pareto improving. Consider then the situation of state B: even if one could somehow calculate the harm done to state B by seeing individuals in state A tortured or discriminated against, and fully compensate state B for it (a difficult exercise discussed above), it goes without saying that this compensation does not help the actual victims of torture or discrimination in state A. How did we get to these absurd comparisons? Because human rights obligations are not so much state-to-state obligations but rather obligations held by state A against individuals *within* the jurisdiction of state A. In this constellation, a liability rule or theory of efficient breach where entitlements and compensation change hands *between* states is wholly inappropriate. The same is true for state entitlements as against individuals under international criminal law. Where human rights impose obligations on states as against their own people; international criminal law imposes obligations on individuals as against states and the world community so as to protect other individuals. To somehow permit Slobodan Milosovic or Saddam Hussein to "buy off" some of their criminal obligations, by paying the state-holders of the related entitlements, not only flies in the face of the moralisms or incommensurability *rationale* for inalienability discussed earlier. It also overlooks the fact that the state-holders of the entitlement not to see Milosovic or Hussein engage in, for example, genocide or crimes against humanity are not the actual beneficiaries of the entitlement. If anything, the individual victims in the former Yugoslavia or Iraq ought to be paid, not the governments of, say, France or the United States.

In sum, the more one regards the ultimate beneficiary of entitlements, or even the actual holder of entitlements, to be individuals or operators within the state (such as individuals protected by human rights or companies protected by trade or investment law), the more difficult it becomes to apply state-to-state liability rules or efficient breach. One must then open the black box of the state and, where liability rules appear otherwise appropriate, consider compensation by states to individuals (as in human rights or investment law) or compensation by individuals to states or other individuals (as in criminal law). As pointed out earlier, however, most of these transfers (in particular, those regarding human rights and international criminal law) ought to be prohibited in the first place as the entitlements involved are optimally protected as inalienable (because of significant externalities, moralisms and/or paternalism).

Let it be clear that the last two reasons in favor of higher protection of international law – states may not be rational utility-maximizers in the first place, nor are they unitary actors – are objections not only against liability protection but also against consensual state-to-state transfers of entitlements under a property rule. There, as well, the consenting states involved may not maximize the country's overall welfare (previous section) or harm individuals or companies within the state (this section).

6 A matrix to decide on how to protect international law entitlements

It was not the goal of this chapter, nor is it the goal of this book, to decide how to protect specific international law entitlements. Rather, this chapter provides one simple rule and a complicated matrix within which negotiators must make this decision for themselves on a treaty-by-treaty and country-by-country basis. The simple rule is that, as in domestic law, by default, entitlements under international law ought to be protected by a property rule. This prescription goes against both the extreme of European absolutism (favoring inalienability across the board) and the extreme of American voluntarism (favoring liability protection across the board). A default rule of property protection is justified by principles of contractual freedom, welfare maximization and the fact that property protection requires the least amount of intervention. Nonetheless, I have offered three arguments to move from property protection to inalienability: (1) significant externalities, (2) moralisms or incommensurability, and

(3) paternalism. Conversely, on the other extreme of the scale of protection, this chapter elaborated three arguments to move from property to liability protection: (1) hold-out, (2) free-load (difficult to apply in the consent-based system of international law) and (3) high transaction costs. In addition, and beyond the criteria offered in the Calabresi and Melamed model itself, three arguments were pointed out that may, or should, in the mind of treaty negotiators tip the balance in favor of a *lower* level of protection: the need for flexibility to attract participation and prevent exit; the consent rule and general uncertainty which may require incomplete contracting and flexibility; and legitimacy concerns. All three of these arguments are also reasons why European absolutism goes, in many cases, too far. Conversely, this chapter also identified five elements which, where they are present, can militate in favor of a *higher* level of protection in international law and make, in particular, liability protection problematic: absence of collective valuation; costs and errors of collective valuation; unique goods and non-monetized exchange; stability and the need to make credible commitments; and inequality between states. All five of these arguments are also reasons why American voluntarism goes, in many cases, too far. At the very least, before treaty negotiators impose a liability rule they must carefully weigh the totality of these valuation, compensation and other costs against any gains that may be made in, for example, transaction costs.[75] Finally, two broader

[75] As Friedman notes, "the efficient breach rule, while designed to reduce transaction costs, fares poorly precisely because of the expensive transactions that it in fact generates": Daniel Friedman, "The Efficient

critiques were offered against this book's broader states-as-rational-actors model which may, in particular, undermine the effective operation of liability rules (even though they also taint property protection): states may not be rational, utility-maximizers and states are not unitary actors.

Table 1 summarizes the proposed matrix. It illustrates how any decision on optimal levels of protection depends on the particular treaty or commitment in question. For example, if non-monetizable values are at stake, inalienability may be called for (moralisms). If, on the other hand, fungible goods are involved, liability protection becomes more attractive (as errors in collective valuation are less likely). Equally, any decision on optimal levels of protection is likely to vary, depending on the state or negotiator making the assessment. For example, liability protection may not be attractive to developing countries which do not have the resources to invoke the take-and-pay principle, or seek strong pre-commitment as against domestic pressure groups. As a result of conflicting demands for how to protect an international commitment, mixed systems may therefore emerge.

Breach Fallacy" (1989), 18 *J Leg Stud* 1, at 2. As was noted in the context of domestic contract law, "parties must balance the benefits from credible commitments against the benefits of flexibility in adjusting to realized states of the world": Robert Scott and Paul Stephan, "Self-Enforcing International Agreements and the Limits of Coercion" (2004), *Wisconsin LR* 551, at 615, note 174.

Table 1 A matrix to decide on how to protect international law entitlements

Arguments for the default rule of PROPERTY PROTECTION	Arguments for deviation toward "higher" protection INALIENABILITY	Arguments for deviation toward "lower" protection LIABILITY PROTECTION
1. Contractual freedom	1. Significant externalities (transfer is necessarily inefficient)	1. Hold-out (strategic behavior by holders of entitlements: they refuse to sell)
2. Welfare maximization	2. Moralisms and Incommensurability (entitlement cannot be monetized)	2. Free-load (strategic behavior by potential buyers of entitlements: they refuse to buy to free-ride on others)
3. Requires least amount of intervention	3. Paternalism (self-paternalism; true paternalism)	3. High transaction costs (making forced transfer with objective valuation more efficient)
	Features favoring "higher" protection 1. Absence of collective valuation 2. Costs and errors in collective valuation 3. Unique goods	**Features favoring "lower" protection** 1. Attract participation and prevent exit in a consent-based system

Table 1 (*cont.*)

Arguments for the default rule of PROPERTY PROTECTION	Arguments for deviation toward "higher" protection INALIENABILITY	Arguments for deviation toward "lower" protection LIABILITY PROTECTION
	4. Stability and the need to make credible commitments 5. Inequalities between states 6. States may not internalize costs or maximize welfare 7. States are not unitary actors	2. Consent rule and uncertainty requiring incomplete contracting and flexibility 3. Legitimacy concerns

5

How are international law entitlements currently protected?

This chapter tests the normative predictions developed in the previous chapter. It looks at whether this book's framework of variable protection of entitlements – based on inalienability, property rules and liability rules – finds application in the formal standards of protection set out in current general international law. The ILC Articles on State Responsibility are used as reflective of this general international law.[1] A limited number of specialized treaty regimes are also tested. As a descriptive matter, or a question of how the law currently is (*lex lata*), both European absolutism and American voluntarism are wrong. International law entitlements are not sacredly protected as inalienable, nor simply protected by a mere liability rule. As predicted, international law is, by default, protected by a property rule. Only in limited circumstances are entitlements made inalienable or protected by liability rules.

[1] Draft Articles on the Responsibility of States for Internationally Wrongful Acts (2001), adopted by the International Law Commission, GAOR 56th Session, Supplement no. 10 (A/56/10) (ILC Articles). These ILC Articles are generally considered to reflect customary international law and/or general principles of law. Even where particular ILC articles or provisions would not reflect custom or general principles of law, in any event they express the wisdom and opinion of a highly qualified and diverse group of international lawyers and, on that ground, are a source of international law in the sense of Article 38.1(c) of the ICJ Statute (referring to "teachings of the most highly qualified publicists of the various nations, as subsidiary means for the determination of rules of law").

1 International law is, in principle, not inalienable

In contrast to the demands of European absolutism, most entitlements under current international law can be transferred, or contracted out from, at will and are, therefore, *not* inalienable. What follow are the default rules of protection of international law entitlements.

First, states have the right to amend treaties by agreement between the parties.[2] Therefore, as between a willing seller and a willing buyer, treaty entitlements can be transferred and are *not* inalienable. Second, states are equally free to contract out of customary international law (in particular the general law of treaties and state responsibility) when crafting new treaties.[3] As *lex specialis* such specific treaty provisions then prevail over the general, fall-back rules of custom which are, therefore, derogable or supplementary, rather than inalienable. Third, besides renegotiating the treaty itself or contracting out of custom, states also have the right to settle specific disputes that arise under a treaty or custom.

[2] Article 39, Vienna Convention on the Law of Treaties, 22 May 1969, entry into force 27 January 1980, 1155 UNTS 331 (VCLT): "A treaty may be amended by agreement between the parties."

[3] See, for example, Article 5 of the VCLT which applies the VCLT (largely considered to reflect customary international law) to treaties adopted within an international organization "without prejudice to any relevant rules of the organization." See also Article 55 of the ILC Articles stating that the ILC Articles do not apply "where and to the extent that the conditions for the existence of an internationally wrongful act or the content or implementation of the international responsibility of a State are governed by special rules of international law."

Crucially, such settlements must not necessarily be consistent with the original treaty or custom. As part of a settlement, the victim of breach can validly consent to the full or partial continuation of what constituted the breach[4] and/or waive its right to invoke responsibility.[5] In sum, international law entitlements are *not* written in stone. States can change the rules, and consent to breach or waive their rights.[6]

A first type of international law entitlement that is, however, inalienable is that protected by what are called peremptory norms of general international law or *jus cogens*. The Vienna Convention on the Law of Treaties defines these norms as those "accepted and recognized by the international community of States as a whole as a norm from which no derogation is permitted." Oft-cited examples are

[4] Article 20, ILC Articles: "Valid consent by a State to the commission of a given act by another State precludes the wrongfulness of that act in relation to the former State to the extent that the act remains within the limits of that consent."

[5] Article 45, ILC Articles: "The responsibility of a State may not be invoked if: (a) The injured State has validly waived the claim . . . "

[6] This is why, in this author's view, WTO members can settle disputes in deviation from the WTO treaty for as long as they do not thereby affect third-party rights. The direction in Article 3.5 of the DSU that all solutions to matters formally raised under the DSU "shall be consistent with [WTO] agreements" is there to protect third parties. It does not prevent the two disputing parties from changing, adapting or dis-applying a particular rule as it applies to the dispute at hand *for as long as third-party rights remain unaffected.* Under the VCLT (Article 30), such settlement prevails over the WTO rule as the norm later in time; under the ILC Articles, the settlement amounts to consent precluding wrongfulness (under Article 20) or, at the least, a waiver of dispute settlement rights (under Article 45).

the prohibitions of slavery, genocide, aggression and crimes against humanity.[7] As is the case for inalienable entitlements in domestic law – such as the prohibition to sell one's kidney – contracting out of *jus cogens* is prohibited and any treaty that conflicts with *jus cogens* is void.[8]

In addition to *jus cogens*, there is a second type of international law entitlement with inalienable features, namely: treaties of a legislative nature that set out so-called collective obligations (such as most human rights or labor conventions and certain environmental treaties). Unlike *jus cogens*, entitlements under those treaties *can* be reallocated by consent of all the parties to the treaty. Treaties, even those of a legislative type (including the UN Charter), can of course be amended. However, given the high and increasing number of parties involved in many of today's regional and multilateral conventions, in practice, even here reallocation by what one could call legislative action has proven extremely difficult. More importantly, like *jus cogens*, once entitlements under collective obligations are allocated by the multilateral treaty, they cannot normally be transferred or modified *inter se* as between two or a sub-set of the parties to

[7] At some point, *jus cogens* (or at least part thereof) was even referred to using the domestic law analogy of "crimes" of state (Article 19, Draft Articles on State Responsibility (1996), UN Doc A/51/10, contrasting crimes of state with mere delicts, see *supra*, Chapter 3 note 3).

[8] Article 53 of the VCLT: "A treaty is void if, at the time of its conclusion, it conflicts with a peremptory norm of general international law." In addition, Article 64 provides: "If a new peremptory norm of general international law emerges, any existing treaty which is in conflict with that norm becomes void and terminates."

the treaty. Bilateral contracting out is, in other words, not permitted (a feature of inalienability). I elaborate further on the difference between collective and bilateral obligations in the next section.

2 International law is, by default, protected by a property rule, not a liability rule

If European absolutism is exaggerated, so is American voluntarism. Indeed, contrary to the claims of American voluntarism, when it comes to the second-order question of how and how strongly international law is currently protected (to be distinguished from the third-order question of back-up enforcement in case the rules of protection are flouted, discussed below in chapter 6), international law represents more than mere pledges. According to the principle of *pacta sunt servanda*, "[e]very treaty in force is binding upon the parties to it and must be performed by them in good faith."[9] In addition, international law entitlements are, by default, protected by the relatively strong regime of property protection, not the weaker regime of mere liability. Put differently, as much as no one can take my house without my agreement, an entitlement under international law cannot be unilaterally taken without the agreement of its holder. Crucially, in both cases, this protection remains even if the taker fully compensates the holder, that is, even if the taker pays me the going price for my house or fully compensates the state for its entitlement to, for example, open trade or clean air. In sum,

[9] Article 26, VCLT.

unless there is mutual agreement, the default rule is that international law cannot be "bought out."

More specifically, as regards past violations, or the retrospective protection of entitlements in those cases where breach has already ceased, the fall-back principle in international law is restitution, *not* compensation.[10] This obligation of restitution – defined as an obligation to "re-establish the situation which existed before the wrongful act was committed"[11] – is only absolved in case, and to the extent that, restitution either (1) is "materially impossible" or (2) "involves a burden out of all proportion to the benefit deriving from restitution instead of compensation."[12] Put differently, where state A confiscates the embassy of state B in violation of the rules on diplomatic immunity,[13] it does not

[10] Article 35, ILC Articles. [11] *Ibid.*

[12] *Ibid.* In the 1996 ILC Draft Articles, a further limit (not withheld in the final 2001 Articles) was mentioned, namely restitution in kind is not obligatory in case it would "seriously jeopardize the political independence or economic stability of the State which has committed the internationally wrongful act, whereas the injured State would not be similarly affected if it did not obtain restitution in kind" (Article 43(d), Draft Articles on State Responsibility (1996), UN Doc A/51/10). A Resolution on Obligations *Erga Omnes* in International Law, adopted in 2005 by the Institute of International Law (available at www.idi-iil.org/idiF/resolutionsF/2005_kra_01_fr.pdf, last visited 17 September 2007), is even stricter in its demand for restitution providing (in Article 2(b)) that "restitution should be effected unless materially impossible." No other excuse is provided for.

[13] Article 22, Vienna Convention on Diplomatic Relations, 14 April 1961, entry into force 24 April 1964, 500 UNTS 95: "1. The premises of the mission shall be inviolable ... 3. The premises of the mission, their furnishings and other property thereon and the means of transport of the

suffice for state A to pay full compensation. Unless such is "materially impossible" or involves a burden for state A "out of all proportion" to the benefit for state B, state A *must* hand the embassy back to state B. In this sense, international law requires specific performance, *not* expectation damages. Efficient breach – or deterring compliance whenever its costs outweigh the benefits – is, therefore, *not* the goal of international law. On the contrary, most efficient breaches will not even be tolerated since restitution that involves a burden with *any* degree of proportion to its benefits remains mandated. Only if such burden is out of *all* proportion can the taker of an entitlement rest with mere compensation.

Crucially, as concerns the future or prospective protection of entitlements in those cases where breach continues, the fall-back principle is, equally, cessation of the breach and a continued duty of performance. In other words, the obligation is specific performance; compensation does not suffice.[14] Apart from consent or waiver by the victim of the breach – possibilities mentioned earlier in support of the proposition that international law is *not* inalienable – there are, under general international law, no exceptions to this obligation of cessation

mission shall be immune from search, requisition, attachment or execution."

[14] Article 29, ILC Articles: "The legal consequences of an internationally wrongful act . . . do not affect the continued duty of the responsible State to perform the obligation breached." Article 30(b) states more explicitly: "The State responsible for the internationally wrongful act is under an obligation . . . to cease that act, if it is continuing." In addition, Article 30(b) even obliges the wrongdoing state "to offer appropriate assurances and guarantees of non-repetition, if the circumstances so require."

or specific performance.[15] Put differently, while tolerance for certain forms of efficient breach could be read in the "burden out of all proportion" language for the obligation of restitution, as regards continuing violations, efficient breach is neither the stated goal, nor ever an excuse for violation. Unless otherwise stipulated, states cannot, therefore, buy their way out of future performance. They *must* perform their obligations.[16]

In sum, making abstraction of *jus cogens*, unless otherwise specified in a specific treaty regime, international law is protected by a property rule, not a liability rule.

As hinted at earlier, precision must be added as regards treaties of a legislative nature such as human rights and labor conventions or certain environmental treaties. Like bilateral agreements, multilateral treaties are, by default, protected by a property rule.[17] However, in such multilateral context the question arises whether two parties to the treaty

[15] This strong presumption in favor of keeping treaties intact, and obliging performance with them, is found also in Article 49.3 of the ILC Articles (even where countermeasures to induce compliance with an obligation are permitted, "[c]ountermeasures shall, as far as possible, be taken in such a way as to permit the resumption of performance of the obligations in question") and in international case law (where courts and tribunals have been extremely reluctant to find the invalidity or termination of treaties, see, for example, Alan Boyle, "The Gabcikovo-Nagymaros Case: New Law in Old Bottles" (1997) 8 *YB Int Env L* 13.

[16] Articles 54–64 of the VCLT (on termination and suspension of the operation of treaties) and Articles 20–27 of the ILC Articles (circumstances precluding wrongfulness) provide limited exceptions in this respect, but have nothing to do with efficient breach or permitting compensation instead of performance.

[17] The VCLT and ILC Articles apply to both bilateral and multilateral treaties.

may agree to modify the treaty only as between themselves (*inter se*), that is, whether one state can agree to transfer its entitlement to, for example, clean air or free trade to another state without the consent of the remaining parties to the treaty? If so, the obligations in question are of a bilateral or reciprocal nature, comparable to a contract. In other situations, however, entitlements under the multilateral treaty cannot be separated into bundles of bilateral obligations but are held collectively by all parties.[18] Such entitlements derive from what is referred to as collective or *erga omnes partes* obligations, comparable to a statute or legislative act.[19] In respect of such collective obligations, international law has limited the possibility for *inter se* transfers or contracting out. This, in effect, strengthens the protection of entitlements under certain multilateral treaties, as it makes it more difficult to change them or to give them away. In that more limited sense, the protection then becomes inalienable.

According to the Vienna Convention on the Law of Treaties, *inter se* modifications of a multilateral treaty are only permitted if either (1) the multilateral treaty provides for such possibility, or (2) the treaty does not prohibit the *inter se* modification, and the modification neither "affect[s] the enjoyment by the other parties of their rights under the [multilateral] treaty or the performance of their obligations,"

[18] Also referred to in Article 48.1(a) of the ILC Articles as obligations "established for the protection of a collective interest of the group" of states party to the treaty (or, for that matter, bound by the custom).

[19] On the difference between collective and bilateral obligations, see Joost Pauwelyn, "A Typology of Multilateral Treaty Obligations: Are WTO Obligations Bilateral or Collective in Nature?" (2003), 14 *EJIL* 907.

nor "relate[s] to a provision, derogation from which is incompatible with the effective execution of the object and purpose of the [multilateral] treaty as a whole." In other words, as collective or *erga omnes partes* entitlements are effectively held by *all* the parties to the treaty (such as entitlements under most human rights or environmental agreements), they can, in principle, only be transferred or modified by agreement of *all* of its holders, not bilaterally as between two states only.[20] In contrast, reciprocal or bilateral entitlements – even those set out in a multilateral treaty, such as the convention on diplomatic relations, most trade agreements or emission credits under the Kyoto Protocol – can be transferred or contracted away *inter se* unless such either (1) is prohibited in the treaty or (2) relates to a provision "derogation from which is incompatible with the effective execution of the object and purpose of the treaty as a whole."

[20] Bringing the obligation close to *jus cogens* status, Article 311 of the UN Convention on the Law of the Sea goes even further and provides that "States Parties agree that there shall be no amendments to the basic principle relating to the common heritage of mankind set forth in article 136 [declaring the sea-bed and ocean floor and subsoil thereof beyond the limits of national jurisdiction, including its resources, to be the 'common heritage of mankind'] and that they shall not be party to any agreement in derogation thereof" (United Nations Convention on the Law of the Sea, 10 December 1982, entry into force 16 November 1994, 1833 UNTS 3 (UNCLOS)). The difference from *jus cogens* is, of course, that Article 311 only applies to UNCLOS parties whilst *jus cogens* by definition applies to all states. See also the UNESCO Universal Declaration on the Human Genome and Human Rights (1997), whose Article 1 declares the following: "The human genome underlies the fundamental unity of all members of the human family, as well as the recognition of their inherent dignity and diversity. In a symbolic sense, it is the heritage of humanity."

In sum, bilateral entitlements are protected by a property rule; collective entitlements are, in principle, inalienable unless all the parties to the multilateral treaty agree to reallocate the entitlement.

3 An evaluation of inalienability in current international law

That international entitlements are not uniformly protected as inalienable meets our prediction. It is, after all, not that surprising except for those who stick to Grotius' definition of international law as natural law which "is unchangeable, even in the sense that it cannot be changed by God." What are more surprising, and contradict this book's framework, are the criteria (or absence thereof) for elevation to *jus cogens* status and the resulting lack of a clear list of *jus cogens* norms.[21] The same is true in respect of collective obligations or treaties of a legislative type.

(a) The need for a more objective analysis

Promoting a norm to *jus cogens* (thereby making it truly inalienable) or to collective obligation status (thereby prohibiting *inter se* transfers, a feature of inalienability) is a

[21] For the very first explicit recognition of a norm as *jus cogens* by the International Court of Justice, see *Case Concerning Armed Activities on the Territory of the Congo (DRC v. Rwanda)*, Jurisdiction and Admissibility, 3 February 2006, available at www.icj-cij.org, at para. 64 (noting that the character of *jus cogens* "is assuredly the case with regard to the prohibition of genocide").

serious decision, with important freedom-restricting and back-up enforcement consequences (the former were discussed in chapter 4; the latter are dealt with below in chapter 6.2). Yet, in international law, little thought is given as to the specific reasons why, and the circumstances of when, such decision ought to be made.[22] Indeed, when it comes to *jus cogens*, current international law offers no criteria at all, other than the tautology that *jus cogens* norms must be "accepted and recognized by the international community of States as a whole as a norm from which no derogation is permitted."[23] Equally, as far as collective obligations are concerned, all we know *lex lata* is that they are "established for the protection of a collective interest of the group"[24] and "must transcend the sphere of bilateral relations of the states parties."[25] The ILC Commentary gives some examples of collective obligations – "they might concern ... the environment or security of a region (e.g., a regional nuclear free zone treaty or a regional

[22] As noted recently by Dinah Shelton: "Although it may be appropriate today to recognize fundamental norms deriving from an international public order, the extensive assertions of peremptory norms made by some writers and international tribunals, without presenting any evidence to support the claimed superior status of the norms under consideration, pose risks for the international legal order and the credibility of the authors and tribunals." Dinah Shelton, "Normative Hierarchy in International Law" (2006), 100 *AJIL* 291, at 292.

[23] See Article 53, VCLT; and also Article 64, VCLT.

[24] See Article 48.1(a), ILC Articles.

[25] Commentaries to the Draft Articles on the Responsibility of States for Internationally Wrongful Acts (2001), GAOR 56th Session, Supplement no. 10 (A/56/10), at 321.

system for the protection of human rights)"[26] – but explicitly states that this list is only illustrative and that "[i]t will be a matter for the interpretation and application of the primary rule to determine into which of the categories an obligation comes."[27] In the absence of further criteria and, worse, a decision-maker with the power to decide which norm gets classified where,[28] there is no accepted list of *jus cogens* or collective obligations. As a result, in many cases, states do not even know which rules are at the pinnacle of legal protection. To make a domestic law analogy, this would be like announcing the creation of a criminal justice system without defining what conduct is criminal in the first place.[29]

Current decisions on inalienability seem predominantly subjective and based almost exclusively on the importance given by major stakeholders to the norm or treaty in question. It is generally agreed, for example, that norms are

[26] *Ibid.*, at 320. [27] *Ibid.*, at 297.

[28] The ICJ has only recently decided in explicit terms that the prohibition of genocide is, indeed, *jus cogens*. See *Case Concerning Armed Activities on the Territory of the Congo (DRC v. Rwanda)*, Jurisdiction and Admissibility, para. 64. Although treaties could, in principle, decide that the obligations set out are either bilateral or collective in nature, very few do so. For an exception, see Article 311 of UNCLOS, quoted *supra* in note 20.

[29] As Sheldon notes, "[*jus cogens*] is a concept that lacks both an agreed content and consensus in state practice" (at 292), and "the concept of *jus cogens* has received widespread support, without any agreement or clarity about its source, content or impact" (at 299): Shelton "Normative Hierarchy in International Law."

elevated to *jus cogens* status based on the important moral or ethical values that they protect.[30] Equally, when it comes to identifying collective obligations, it has become a badge of honor for a treaty to qualify, and almost a defeat or relegation for the values pursued when a treaty is found to set out "merely" bilateral or reciprocal obligations.[31]

[30] Alfred Verdross, who introduced the notion of *jus cogens* in a 1937 article, refers to general principles of morality or public policy "common to the juridical orders of all civilized nations": Alfred Verdross, "Forbidden Treaties in International Law" (1937), 31 *AJIL* 571, at 572. In a later article, Verdross went as far as stating that "all rules of general international law created for a humanitarian purpose" constitute *jus cogens*: Alfred Verdross, "Jus Dispositivum and Jus Cogens in International Law" (1966), 60 *AJIL* 55, at 59. See also Prosper Weil, "Towards Relative Normativity in International Law" (1983), 77 *AJIL* 413 footnote 29 ("Such terms as 'legal conscience of states', 'awakening of conscience', 'universal conscience', 'common good of mankind' recur like a leitmotiv on practically every page of the International Law Commission's work on the theories of *jus cogens* and international crimes"), and Jonathan Charney, "Universal International Law" (1993), 87 *AJIL* 529, at 541 (*jus cogens* "is distinguished from ordinary international law because it is based on natural law propositions applicable to all legal systems, all persons, or the system of international law"). The Resolution on Obligations *Erga Omnes* in International Law (2005) of the Institute of International Law explains the status of *jus cogens* with reference to "fundamental values of the international community" (Second preambular paragraph).

[31] In respect of WTO obligations, see Chios Charmody, "WTO Obligations as Collective" (2006), 17 *EJIL* 419, and Sungjoon Cho, "The Nature of Remedies in International Trade Law" (2004), 65 *U Pittsburgh LR* 763. In a similar vein, the Resolution on Obligations *Erga Omnes* in International Law of the Institute of International Law (2005) defines

What this book's framework adds, then, is a more objective assessment of when to make entitlements inalienable. Although the model may add relatively little for the question of when to qualify norms as *jus cogens* – most, if not all, of *jus cogens* entitlements can be explained based on the moralisms or incommensurability ground for inalienability discussed earlier – even there it offers an alternative and arguably more objective justification for promoting a norm to *jus cogens*: where it is difficult, if not impossible, to put a price on an entitlement (to, for example, freedom or the survival of an ethnic group), transfer cannot increase welfare. As a result, it makes sense to ban it completely, i.e., to make the entitlement inalienable. From this perspective, international law rightly bans slavery, genocide, aggression and crimes against humanity as *jus cogens* since it is impossible, even inappropriate, to monetize the value of the entitlements protected by these norms.[32] Put differently, looked at through the lens of this book's framework, what makes a norm *jus cogens* is not so much that it reflects hierarchically superior or more important, universal values; but rather that it involves entitlements which, for one reason or another, raise the problem of incommensurability.

collective or *erga omnes partes* obligations "in view of their common values and concern for compliance" (Article 1(b)).

32 Yet, see the original argument against slavery by Adam Smith, offered in the eighteenth century at a time when slavery and slave trading was still perfectly legal: "the work done by freemen comes cheaper in the end than that performed by slaves." Quoted in Niall Ferguson, *Empire* (London: Basic Books, 2004), at 96.

(b) *Collective obligations through the lens of externalities, incommensurability and paternalism*

When it comes to selecting the second type of inalienable entitlements, namely collective obligations – an exercise with great practical importance[33] but discussed far less than *jus cogens* – the model proposed in this book offers deeper insights. Applying the three specific reasons to make entitlements inalienable (significant externalities, incommensurability and paternalism), moralisms, or the problem of incommensurability, can explain why most human rights conventions set out collective obligations which cannot be transferred *inter se*. As noted earlier, significant externalities may justify the label of collective obligation for disarmament and certain environmental obligations, especially those concerning global commons. Where an activity creates such a high degree of externalities – say, dropping a nuclear bomb or wide-scale, cross-border pollution – no one might be willing or able to pay for all the costs related to the transfer of the entitlement. Hence, it may be more efficient to ban the transfer in the first place. The Antarctic Treaty prohibits, for example, nuclear explosions and disposal of radioactive and

[33] Distinguishing collective from bilateral obligations is important not only for the permissibility of *inter se* modifications but also for the question of standing and the permissibility of *inter se* suspension as a form of countermeasure for a breach of other obligations or bilateral settlements of disputes that deviate from the multilateral treaty. See Joost Pauwelyn, "A Typology of Multilateral Treaty Obligations: Are WTO Obligations Bilateral or Collective in Nature?" (2003), 14 *EJIL* 907, at 908–9.

chemical wastes as well as the testing of any type of weapons in Antarctica.[34] Similarly, the Partial Test Ban Treaty prohibits nuclear weapon tests in the places defined by the treaty, such as outer space and the high seas.[35] Paternalism (of the minor–adult sort) may, in turn, justify making collective obligations where occupied territories or failed states are involved, both being actors operating from a position of weakness. The Fourth Geneva Convention, for example, prohibits protected persons and occupied territories from renouncing or transferring any of the rights granted to them in the convention.[36]

Crucially, pursuant to the model of variable protection developed in this book, whether an entitlement is

[34] Article I(1), Antarctic Treaty, 1 December 1959, entry into force 23 June 1961, 402 UNTS 71.

[35] Treaty Banning Nuclear Weapon Tests in the Atmosphere, in Outer Space and Under Water, 5 August 1963, entry into force 10 October 1963, 480 UNTS 43.

[36] Article 7 of the Fourth Geneva Convention provides that protected persons, who include those in occupied territories, "may in no circumstances renounce in part or in entirety the rights secured to them by the present Convention." Article 47 reiterates and expands upon this injunction: "Protected persons who are in occupied territory shall not be deprived, in any case or in any manner whatsoever, of the benefits of the present Convention by any change introduced, as the result of the occupation of a territory, into the institutions or government of the said territory, *nor by any agreement concluded between the authorities of the occupied territories and the Occupying Power*, nor by any annexation by the latter of the whole or part of the occupied territory" (emphasis added). Geneva Convention (IV) Relative to the Protection of Civilian Persons in Time of War, 12 August 1949, entry into force 21 October 1950, 75 UNTS 287.

protected as inalienable, property or under a liability rule does not say anything about the subjective importance of the treaty or the objectives that it pursues. Instead, what counts under the model is the maximization of welfare (broadly defined). Let us take the example of global warming. Few today dispute that this is an important issue and raises global concerns which transcend the individual interests of states. Following the ILC definition of collective obligations, one could, therefore, be tempted to label "entitlements" to emit a certain level of greenhouse gases as corresponding to collective obligations which, in the words of the ILC, pursue "a collective interest of the group."[37] On that ground one could then decide to make these entitlements inalienable. However, inalienability simply because of the importance of the cause or the collectivity of the interests concerned may not be the best or most efficient way to deal with global warming. And this is, after all, what the treaty wants to do: combat global warming at, one would presume, the lowest cost. Indeed, notwithstanding the importance of the goal pursued, property protection may be better. This is exactly what the Kyoto Protocol does. The core advantage of permitting Kyoto parties to trade emission credits, that is, the "entitlement" to emit a certain level of greenhouse gases (under a property system), is economic efficiency. Where emissions automatically affect all countries (as in global warming) and abatement costs vary between countries and industries, a system of tradable quantity limits will obtain a given level of abatement at the lowest possible cost. As Wiener explains, in such a system

[37] Article 48.1(a), ILC Articles.

"[e]ach source abates up to the point that its marginal cost of abatement equals the market price for an allowance to cover the next unit of emissions. High-cost abaters undertake less abatement and buy more allowances; low-cost abaters undertake more abatement and sell allowances."[38] In sum, polluting combined with buying emission allowances from someone who can abate more cheaply than you can maximize welfare without increasing overall levels of emissions.[39]

Equally, advocates of making WTO entitlements inalienable (as in collective obligations) ought to think twice. That liberalized trade is an important objective which can boost economies worldwide and lift millions out of poverty is not a sufficient reason to prevent WTO members from *inter se* transfers. As with global warming, protecting entitlements as property, instead of inalienability, does not somehow degrade the objective pursued. If welfare maximization (broadly defined) is the goal, it may be better to permit countries to contract out of WTO obligations for as long as they do not affect third-party rights (such as the most-favored-nation principle). Such consensual reintroduction of trade restrictions, between a willing buyer and a willing seller (for whatever reason, be it human rights, cultural diversity or to combat conflict diamonds) must be presumed to maximize welfare and to be Pareto superior, especially if third parties are kept unharmed. If, in contrast, all WTO entitlements were written

[38] Jonathan Wiener, "Global Environmental Regulation: Instrument Choice in Legal Context" (1999), 108 *Yale LJ* 677, at 715.

[39] For a critique, see Michael J. Sandel, Editorial, "It's Immoral To Buy the Right To Pollute," *NY Times*, 15 December 1997, at A23; and "Sins of Emission," *The Economist, 5–11 August* 2006, at 15.

in stone and could only be altered with the consent of *all* WTO members (an event that is increasingly unlikely with 152 WTO members and counting), a serious loss in contractual freedom to address wide diversities between WTO members would result. Such loss would not only reduce the policy space of WTO members but also prevent welfare maximization. After all, unlike many human rights entitlements,[40] most trade entitlements can be monetized and there is no issue of moralisms. Trade is an instrument that creates welfare, which, in turn, permits the pursuit of other values. Trade is not an end in itself. To put a price on it (as is regularly done for investments in NAFTA and BITs) is, in other words, possible and appropriate. Only where transfer of WTO entitlements would create externalities that are so grave as to prevent an increase in welfare (any benefit to be derived by the buyer could not possibly cover the overall cost) ought inalienability (as in collective obligations) to be considered.

In addition, some countries may want to invoke self-paternalism – that is, the need to tie their own hands to resist future temptations of protectionism – to argue for inalienability of certain WTO entitlements. Along similar lines, a

[40] But note that the formal remedy of last resort before, for example, the European Court of Human Rights is compensation or "just satisfaction." Article 41 of the Convention provides as follows: "If the Court finds that there has been a violation of the Convention or the protocols thereto, and if the internal law of the High Contracting Party concerned allows only partial reparation to be made, the Court shall, if necessary, afford just satisfaction to the injured party." This implies that the Court does, in one way or another, put a price on breach of human rights.

complaint often heard by weaker countries is that bigger players "force" them into bilateral agreements either to *detract* from earlier multilateral agreements (such as the bilateral non-surrender agreements pushed for by the United States to shield US nationals from the Statute of the ICC), or to *add* to earlier multilateral agreements (such as regional trade deals concluded by the United States or Europe where developing countries are "forced" into TRIPS-plus commitments). Out of self-paternalism – that is, so as to tie their own hands to the earlier multilateral agreement – one way to deal with such complaints could be to make the entitlements under the multilateral agreement inalienable or, at least, derogeable only within the multilateral framework. This way, weaker countries would stop themselves from too easily selling off their hard-fought-for multilateral entitlements in some subsequent bilateral deal.

A similar, though unsuccessful, attempt was made in the 1970s in respect of the rights of states to their natural resources. As part of a so-called New International Economic Order, developing countries passed resolutions, charters and declarations at the UN General Assembly proclaiming the "full permanent sovereignty of every State over its natural resources and all economic activities" and stating that "[n]o state may be subjected to economic, political or any type of coercion to prevent the free and full exercise of this *inalienable right*."[41] In subsequent investment arbitrations,

[41] *Declaration on the Establishment of a New International Economic Order*, 1 May 1974, A/RES/3201 (S-VI), paragraph (e), emphasis added. See also the *Charter of Economic Rights and Duties of States*, 12 December

however, developing countries which had nationalized foreign companies or otherwise breached contracts with foreign investors were unable to convince the tribunal that a state's rights over its natural resources are part of *jus cogens* or otherwise inalienable.[42]

In any event, possible gains from making an entitlement inalienable must be carefully weighed against the losses in contractual freedom and welfare maximization that come with inalienability.

4 An evaluation of liability rules in current international law

As predicted in chapter 4, in the international context, property protection is the rule, liability protection the exception. As with *jus cogens* and collective obligations (inalienability) discussed earlier, more thought must be given, however, as to precisely when and why to introduce liability rules. The framework of variable protection proposed in this book offers several reasons to move from

1974, A/RES/3281 (XXIX), Article 2.1 ("Every State has and shall freely exercise *full permanent sovereignty*, including possession, use and disposal, over all its wealth, natural resources and economic activities," emphasis added).

42 See, for example, *Kuwait v. Aminoil*, Award of 24 March 1982, 21 ILM 976 (1982), para. 90 ("Equally on the public international law plane it has been claimed that permanent sovereignty over natural resources has become an imperative rule of *ius cogens* prohibiting States from affording, by contract or by treaty, guarantees of any kind against the exercise of the public authority in regard to all matters relating to natural riches. This contention lacks all foundation").

property to liability protection, in particular hold-out and high transaction costs. As noted earlier, given the consent-based system of international law, resolving free-load through liability rules is, however, more difficult: without the consent of the free-riders, international law cannot normally impose liability rules such as taxation or an obligation to pay compensation. As importantly, whenever treaty negotiators consider a liability rule they must take account of the seven features set out earlier that may militate for a level of protection that is higher than mere liability protection (absence of collective valuation; costs and errors of collective valuation; unique goods; stability and the need to make credible commitments; inequality between states; states not acting as welfare-maximizers and states as non-unitary actors).

Examples of current liability rules in international law can be found in the regimes on cross-border environmental damage, the GATT/WTO, NAFTA Chapter 11 and bilateral investment treaties (BITs), all of which are discussed below. The Kyoto Protocol also has features of liability protection. Although its core mechanism – consensual trades of emission credits – amounts to property protection, to some extent Kyoto parties can also exceed their ceiling without a consensual transfer of emission allowances, namely by financing climate-friendly projects in developing countries under the so-called Clean Development Mechanism (CDM) or planting forests which are subsequently discounted as so-called sinks.[43] Although such projects are multilaterally controlled, Kyoto

[43] Article 12, Kyoto Protocol.

parties can thereby emit subject only to making a payment, a pollute-but-pay option that has liability features. Although its success is not guaranteed, the Kyoto Protocol's CDM is facilitated through strict multilateral scrutiny by Kyoto organs and thereby addresses the core problems of collective valuation, stability and credible commitment. Since the mechanism involves a money-transfer from developed countries (buying emission reductions) to developing countries (selling emission reductions), the system also addresses the concern of inequality between states.

(a) Cross-border environmental damage

The closest analogy to liability protection based on high transaction costs in international law – remember Calabresi and Melamed's example of car accidents – is liability for cross-border environmental damage. As much as domestic law does not ban cars because they may cause injury, international law does not prohibit all activities that may cause cross-border damage. On the contrary, the traditional (but much contested) starting point set out in the *Lotus* case is that, especially when it comes to conduct within their own territory, states are legally free to act as they please unless there is a rule of international law that states otherwise.[44] That is how entitlements under international law were at least originally allocated. So how does international law subsequently address activities that may cause cross-border damage? With the exception of certain damage to

[44] *SS Lotus*, PCIJ Series A no. 10 (1927).

global commons in, for example, Antarctica or outer space (addressed earlier in the discussion of collective obligations with inalienable features), international law does not generally prohibit risky activities. Instead, international law regulates such activities through a combination of liability rules aimed at limiting and recovering damages, and property rules aimed at controlling the activity in the first place and preventing injury. When it comes to the production of nuclear energy, for example, the Paris and Vienna Conventions[45] do not prohibit the generation of nuclear energy, but impose strict liability on the operator of a nuclear activity for any damage caused by a nuclear incident. Strict liability of one pre-determined actor namely the operator (not requiring any proof of fault or negligence and avoiding complicated cross-actions) as well as the obligation to take out insurance and financial security for the payment of compensation are crucial features that make the liability rule operational. Accidental damage caused by other ultra-hazardous activities is similarly regulated through liability-type rules in a variety of conventions on, for example, space activities and maritime oil transportation.[46] Transboundary damage arising from "normal" industrial and technical activities, generally characterized as chronic cross-border pollution via air, water or land use, is the focus of the UN International Law Commission (ILC) work on what is called "International Liability for Injurious

[45] Paris Convention on Third Party Liability in the Field of Nuclear Energy, 29 July 1960, 956 UNTS 251, and Vienna Convention on Civil Liability for Nuclear Damage, 21 May 1963, 1063 UNTS 265.

[46] Xue Hanqin, *Transboundary Damage in International Law* (Cambridge: Cambridge University Press, 2003), at 45–72.

Consequences Arising out of Acts not Prohibited by International Law."[47] Like the ultra-hazardous activities mentioned earlier (e.g., nuclear energy), other activities that cause cross-border air or water pollution are not prohibited or illegal. To impose property protection in this type of situation would prevent too many risky but overall desirable activities. Instead, international law imposes a combination of liability rules[48] supplemented by obligations to prevent harm,[49] to seek prior authorization and consultations and to conduct risk assessments and enact certain precautionary measures.[50] The 2001 ILC Draft Articles on *Prevention of Transboundary Harm from Hazardous Activities*[51] applying to "activities not prohibited by international law" (Article 1), impose, for example, an obligation on states "to take all appropriate measures to

[47] See Alan Boyle, "Codification of International Environmental Law and the International Law Commission: Injurious Consequences Revisited," in Alan Boyle and David Freestone (eds.), *International Law and Sustainable Development: Past Achievements and Future Challenges* (Oxford: Oxford University Press, 1999).

[48] See, for example, the Convention on Civil Liability for Damage Resulting from Activities Dangerous to the Environment, 21 June 1993 (not in force) 150 ETS.

[49] Referring to the famous *Trail Smelter* arbitration (3 UNRIAA 1938, [1965]), Kiss and Shelton detect "a general duty on the part of a state to protect other states from injurious acts by individuals within its jurisdiction": Alexandre Kiss and Dinah Shelton, *International Environmental Law*, 3rd edn (Cambridge: Transnational Publishers, 2004), at 184).

[50] *Ibid.*, at 188–223.

[51] Draft Articles on Prevention of Transboundary Harm from Hazardous Activities (2001), adopted by the International Law Commission, GAOR 56th Session, Supplement No. 10 (A/56/10), ch. V.E.1.

prevent significant transboundary harm or at any event to minimize the risk thereof" (Article 3), to "require prior authorization" (Article 6) and to "enter into consultations" (Article 9). In her 2003 book on transboundary damage in international law, Xue Hanqin aptly summed up the overall tension between liability and property protection as follows:

> In essence, we are still struggling with the question of the right to carry certain activities and the duty not to harm. If we put the liability theory in absolute terms, we may reach the conclusion that the source State is permitted to undertake the activity, provided it pays its way. In the final analysis, this means that the source State can do whatever it deems appropriate and necessary, provided it is not forbidden by international law and as long as it can afford to pay damages. This, of course, contravenes the policy goal of the rule as originally envisaged. Even for specially categorized activities, such as ultra-hazardous operations, for example, nuclear energy uses ... permission to act does not mean that their injurious consequences are justifiable as long as they are compensated. They are excusable by the law only in the sense that current human capabilities cannot control them ... The duty to compensate is part of the balancing, but not the sole condition for the permission to carry out ultra-hazardous activities. The ultimate goal is to prevent damage to the greatest extent possible, improving and increasing preventive measures as human capacity to do so develops.[52]

[52] Xue Hanqin, *Transboundary Damage in International Law*, at 315–16.

(b) *Liability rules in the GATT/WTO*

For whatever reason (including purely protectionist pressures), WTO members have the right to unilaterally reintroduce tariffs on imported goods (pursuant to GATT Article XXVIII) or certain restrictions on trade in services (pursuant to GATS Article XXI[53]) on condition that they pay compensation or suffer equivalent suspensions of concessions by other affected WTO members. Although WTO members must first attempt to reach agreement on such proposed changes (a requirement of property protection), in the event no agreement is found, the WTO member requesting the change can enact it unilaterally (that is, unilaterally take entitlements from other members) subject only to a collectively set compensation, namely "compensatory adjustments" set by arbitration[54] or the suspension by other members of "substantially equivalent" concessions or benefits.[55] A similar liability rule applies where a WTO member is faced with a sudden surge in imports resulting from GATT liberalization commitments and is given the right to impose a so-called safeguard (pursuant to GATT Article XIX). In a first instance, WTO members are asked to work out a deal "to maintain a substantially equivalent level of concessions and other

[53] See *supra*, chapter 4 note 13.

[54] Article XXI:3(a), General Agreement on Trade in Services, 15 April 1994, entry into force 1 January 1995, 1869 UNTS 183 (GATS).

[55] Article XXVIII:3(a), General Agreement on Tariffs and Trade, 15 April 1994, entry into force 1 January 1995, 1867 UNTS 187 (GATT), and Article XXI:4(b), GATS.

obligations."[56] Such a deal may include an "adequate means of trade compensation for the adverse effects of the measure [i.e., the safeguard] on their trade." Yet, if no deal can be reached, the safeguard can, nonetheless, be unilaterally imposed, but affected WTO members have the right to suspend "the application of substantially equivalent concessions or other obligations under GATT 1994."[57] If the safeguard responds to an absolute increase in imports and conforms to the provisions in the Safeguards Agreement, however, such equivalent suspension can only be exercised three years after the safeguard was first imposed.[58] Also in the WTO agreement on intellectual property rights (TRIPS) there is an example of liability protection: in limited circumstances, WTO members can issue so-called compulsory licenses even without the consent of the patent holder, subject to the payment of "adequate remuneration."[59]

Two other instances exist where WTO members can engage in certain conduct that is condemned (yet, not unlawful) if only they "pay for it": first, the provision of so-called "actionable subsidies" which are not prohibited but for which the remedy is either to withdraw the subsidy or "to remove the adverse effects" of the subsidy;[60] second, conduct which does not violate WTO rules but nonetheless nullifies

[56] Article 8.1, Agreement on Safeguards, 15 April 1994, entry into force 1 January 1995, 1869 UNTS 154 (SG Agreement).

[57] SG Article 8.2. [58] SG Article 8.3.

[59] Article 31(f), Agreement on Trade Related Intellectual Property Rights, 15 April 1994, entry into force 1 January 1995, 1869 UNTS 299 (TRIPS Agreement).

[60] Article 7.8 of the Subsidies Agreement.

or impairs another member's legitimately expected benefits under a so-called non-violation complaint (pursuant to GATT Article XXIII:1(b)). Here as well, the remedy is not cessation or specific performance, as there is no violation in the first place, but rather the obligation to "make a mutually satisfactory adjustment,"[61] for which arbitration is made available to objectively assess the level of benefits that have been nullified or impaired.[62] In both of these cases (actionable subsidies and non-violation complaints), the payment of compensation – i.e., "removing the adverse effects" or offering a "mutually satisfactory adjustment" – brings the case to a close, as one expects under liability protection. This is unlike compensation or retaliation following a finding of WTO violation under the DSU. In those cases of genuine breach or property protection (discussed below), the remedy of compensation or retaliation is only temporary, with mutually acceptable settlement or compliance/specific performance as the ultimate goal and the only elements that can genuinely close the case.

Each of these liability rules – tariff renegotiations under GATT, change in specific commitments under GATS, safeguards, compulsory licenses, actionable subsidies and non-violation complaints – can be explained within the framework proposed in this book. Forcing WTO members to obtain the agreement of all 151 other WTO members before they can increase tariffs or modify their specific commitments under GATS (as would be the case under property protection) risks hold-outs and implies high, if not

[61] DSU Article 26:1(b). [62] DSU Article 26:1(c).

prohibitive, transaction costs. In addition, the WTO treaty is a standard example of incomplete contracting.[63] Trade negotiators cannot foresee all possible situations, nor can they predict future economic and political developments, both at home and internationally. As a result of this uncertainty, they wanted the flexibility of a liability rule.[64] In the increasingly contentious field of trade regulation, liability protection may also offer a welcome democratic safety-valve. For example, actionable subsidies and conduct that impairs legitimate expectations of other members in line with a non-violation complaint must be "paid for"; however, it is not outright prohibited. Finally, and not least importantly, liability protection in the GATT/WTO system was made possible by an increasingly effective dispute settlement system enabling definitive findings of breach and collective valuation through binding arbitration in an area where entitlements can generally be monetized.

Yet, to label the reintroduction of tariffs, services restrictions or safeguards combined, each time, with equivalent suspensions of concessions by other WTO members as "efficient breach" goes too far.[65] First of all, the reintroduction of trade restrictions in each of those cases is explicitly permitted. Hence, the conduct is intra- not extra-contractual and one

[63] See Henrik Horn, Giovanni Maggi and Robert W. Staiger, "The GATT/WTO as an Incomplete Contract," mimeo, 2006 (available at www.econ-law.se/HMS-5April2006.pdf, last visited 17 September 2007).

[64] See *supra*, chapter 4 notes 30 and 32.

[65] But see Warren Schwartz and Alan Sykes, "The Economic Structure of Renegotiation and Dispute Resolution in the World Trade Organization" (2002), 31 *J Leg Stud* 179.

cannot talk of breach. Second, and more importantly, even if one calls it breach, it is not efficient in any economic sense as no damages for past or future harm must be offered. At best, the *status quo ante* is reached: in response to one party reverting to an earlier, pre-negotiation tariff, the other party can do the same. In none of these situations can one speak of expectation damages that fully compensate the victim, a crucial condition for breach to be efficient. Indeed, unless the country is large enough (and can therefore improve its terms of trade with higher tariffs), retaliation by the original victim of the breach normally causes additional harm to the victim, rather than compensating it. Moreover, as noted earlier, when piercing the state veil, a higher tariff on, for example, steel even combined with compensation or retaliation in some other sector (say, oranges or textiles) does not compensate the losses of steel exporters. From their perspective, the situation is not Pareto improving.

Although some controversy remains on the issue,[66] all WTO commitments other than tariffs, specific commitments

[66] In support of the DSU as a liability regime, see *ibid.*; Robert Lawrence, "Crimes and Punishments? Retaliation under the WTO" (Washington, DC: Peterson Institute, 2003); and David Palmeter and Stanimir Alexandrov, "'Inducing Compliance' with WTO Dispute Settlement," in Daniel Kennedy and James Southwick (eds.), *The Political Economy of International Trade Law: Essays in Honour of Robert Hudec* (Cambridge: Cambridge University Press, 2002), 646. In support of the DSU as a property regime, see John Jackson, "International Law Status of WTO Dispute Settlement Reports: Obligation to Comply or Option to 'Buy Out'?" (2004), 98 *AJIL* 109; Jide Nzelibe, "The Credibility Imperative: The Political Dynamics of Retaliation in the WTO's Dispute Resolution Mechanism" (2005), 6 *Theoretical Inquiries in Law*

in trade in services and those that can be suspended by a safeguard – in particular commitments that are not set out in country-specific schedules of concessions and newer ones such as those on health measures and technical barriers to trade – are protected by a property rule. Such property protection is ensured under the WTO dispute settlement system, where breach can only be cured by either compliance[67] or a settlement;[68] compensation and retaliation are explicitly stated to be "temporary measures."[69] Or as Reto Malacrida, a lawyer working for the WTO secretariat, put it recently: "While the immediate aim of WTO retaliation is re-balancing, its ultimate aim is to induce compliance."[70] This proves that levels of protection need not be uniform across a treaty regime: some commitments may be better protected as property (such as treaty provisions equally applicable to all WTO members), others under a liability rule (such as member-specific commitments set out in schedules that differ for each WTO member). The specific renegotiation schemes that permit the unilateral taking of entitlements only apply for

215; and Joel P. Trachtman, "Building the WTO Cathedral" (2006), available at http://ssrn.com/abstract=815844.

[67] DSU Article 19.1 specifies that following a finding of violation under a WTO agreement, WTO panels/the Appellate Body must recommend that "the Member concerned bring the measure into conformity with that agreement." See also the DSU provisions quoted *infra* note 71.

[68] DSU Article 3.7 ("A solution mutually acceptable to the parties to a dispute and consistent with the covered agreements is clearly to be preferred").

[69] DSU Article 22.1.

[70] Reto Malacrida, "Towards Sounder and Fairer WTO Retaliation" (2008), 42 *Journal of World Trade* 3, at 5.

tariffs, specific services commitments and import surges due to GATT commitments. In the absence of such explicit contracting-out, for other WTO commitments, the default rule of property protection under general international law applies. This property rule is (at least implicitly) confirmed in the WTO's dispute settlement provisions (DSU).[71] WTO arbitrators, in turn, confirmed that the objective of trade retaliation is to induce performance, not to compensate or rebalance the scales.[72] As one recent arbitration panel put it: "we do not read anything in the DSU or in the [Subsidies] Agreement which would create a right not to comply with DSB

[71] See DSU Articles 3, 21 and 22 as elaborated in Jackson, "International Law Status of WTO Dispute Settlement Reports" (Article 3.7: "the first objective of the dispute settlement mechanism is usually to secure the withdrawal of the measures concerned if these are found to be inconsistent"; Article 21.1: "Prompt compliance ... is essential"; Article 22.1: "Compensation and the suspension of concessions ... are temporary measures ... neither ... is preferred to full implementation"; Article 22.8: "The suspension of concessions ... shall be temporary and shall only be applied until such time as the measure found to be inconsistent ... has been removed ... or a mutually satisfactory solution is reached"). In support: Peter Van den Bossche, *The Law and Policy of the WTO* (Cambridge: Cambridge University Press, 2005), at 220 ("The DSU leaves no doubt that compensation and/or the suspension of concessions or other obligations are *not* alternative remedies ... *instead of* complying with the recommendations and rulings," emphasis in original), and Petros Mavroidis, "Remedies in the WTO Legal System: Between a Rock and a Hard Place" (2000), 11 *EJIL* (2000) 763, at 800 (even with compensation or suspensions in place "the WTO member author of the illegal act continues the illegality and has not fulfilled its international obligations").

[72] See, for example, *EC – Bananas*, and *EC – Hormones*.

recommendations and rulings."[73] Crucially, not a single WTO member, not even the United States, has ever argued that compensation or retaliation can fully replace performance as an equally available option, the way proponents of an overall WTO liability scheme suggest.[74] For those WTO

[73] *Canada – Aircraft Credits and Guarantees*, para. 3.104.

[74] In a GAO Report to the Committee on Ways and Means, it is said that "The United States maintains that it has the right not to comply with WTO rulings": United States General Accounting Office, "Report to the Chairman, Committee on Ways and Means, House of Representatives, World Trade Organization: Issues in Dispute Settlement" (August 2000), at 16. Yet, this statement is made in the context of whether WTO rulings have direct effect in the domestic US legal system. It is clear that WTO rulings cannot be enforced in US courts and that, under domestic US law, the US has, indeed, no obligation to comply with WTO rulings. See USTR Press Release, "State Sovereignty and Trade Agreements: The Facts," 14 April 2005, at www.ustr.gov/assets/Document_Library/Fact_Sheets/2005/asset_upload_file870_7578.pdf (last visited 17 September 2007): "WTO, NAFTA and other trade agreements do not in any way preempt or invalidate federal, state, or local laws that may be inconsistent with those agreements. This is because, while the United States has committed itself to adhere to the rules set out in the WTO and the NAFTA agreements, those rules do not automatically override any domestic laws." The same is true in the EC (*Portugal v. Council*, C-149/96, 23 November 1999). The question addressed in this book, however, is whether the United States has an obligation under international law (not US domestic law) to comply with WTO rulings. The answer is yes, subject to the *temporary* alternatives of compensation and trade retaliation. As the same GAO report points out (at p. 15): "Under WTO dispute settlement rules, compliance is the preferred way of responding to an adverse WTO ruling. However, a member may decide not to comply and either offer equivalent compensation or face foreign retaliation. These options, which are considered under the dispute settlement rules to be *temporary*, were designed to protect sovereignty" (emphasis added).

commitments, WTO members are, in other words, obliged to comply with WTO rules or obtain the consent of relevant WTO members to deviate from those rules. They cannot unilaterally take these entitlements, pay compensation for them, and thereby end the matter.[75]

This insistence on property protection, dormant in the original GATT[76] but more explicitly confirmed in the WTO, can, once again, be explained under the matrix proposed in this book. Given the increased complexity of trade rules, WTO members had to weigh the advantages of flexibility offered by a liability rule, against the need for credible

[75] Tellingly, a dispute remains on the agenda of each and every session of the Dispute Settlement Body for surveillance even after retaliation has been approved and this "until the issue is resolved" (DSU Article 21.6).

[76] See GATT Article XXIII:2, which sets up the GATT's dispute settlement process with suspension of concessions by the victim as "appropriate in the circumstances" as a last resort. Although it does not explicitly say so, suspension in Article XXIII:2 reads more like a last resort remedy or sanction to induce performance, rather than a simple replacement or payment for the taking of entitlements. For example, unlike Articles XXVIII (tariff renegotiations) and XIX (safeguards), Article XXIII:2 limits suspension to cases where "circumstances are serious enough" and subjects suspension in response to breach to collective approval. Article XXIII:2 also immediately adds that in response to suspension, a wrongdoer "shall be free, not later than sixty days after such action is taken, to give written notice . . . of its intention to withdraw" from the GATT. In other words, suspension is hardly put up as a normal event or instrument to enable, let alone promote, efficient breach. As explained below (chapter 6.1), the fact that suspension needed to be proportional (although in GATT, the requirement was somewhat broader, namely "appropriate in the circumstances") does not automatically mean that the system is a liability rule. Proportional countermeasures can be appropriate back-up enforcement for a property rule.

commitment and stability which is better served under a property rule. The number of GATT/WTO members has also increased exponentially, from 23 in 1947 to 152 in 2008, making full compensation of potentially 15 other parties increasingly difficult both financially and politically. In addition, with developing countries now constituting the large majority of WTO members, the problems related to liability protection in the presence of huge imbalances of power between players became more acute. More complicated trade commitments also increase the cost and possible errors of collective valuation as is required under liability protection.[77] Finally, as trade commitments evolved from purely state-to-state affairs to rules whose main beneficiaries are seen as private business and traders,[78] compensation and retaliation as equal alternatives to performance became politically less palatable. For example, more exports for US machinery producers (thanks to a compensatory tariff reduction by the EC) do not compensate US farmers kept out of the EC market by a WTO-inconsistent ban on GMOs. Equally, US orange and textiles producers (targeted by EC retaliation in response to a

[77] Robert Scott and Paul Stephan (*The Limits of Leviathan* [Cambridge: Cambridge University Press, 2006]), for example, argue against compensation awards, which are inherent in liability schemes, for international commitments that are non-verifiable, that is, whose control requires information that cannot be proven to a third party at a reasonable cost (at 376). In their view, "[t]he evidence suggests that an attempt to extend formal enforcement to nonverifiable contract terms – such as the obligation to adjust terms in good faith – is likely to impair the efficacy of those informal means of enforcement that rely on reciprocity norms" (at 176–7).

[78] See Panel Report on *US – Section 301*.

WTO-inconsistent tariff on steel imports) are unwilling to pay for benefits that protection may offer to US steel producers. As many of these factors apply also to tariff renegotiations, modification of GATS-specific commitments and safeguards, they can also explain why, in practice, GATT/WTO liability rules have not often been invoked, and decreasingly so over time.[79] In exceptional situations, however, such as in the recent *US – Gambling* dispute discussed earlier,[80] they continue to offer welcome safety valves and flexibility. Yet, focusing on the democratic safety valve offered under liability protection, one might question whether it continues to make sense to protect tariff commitments under a flexible liability rule (GATT Article XXVIII), whereas politically and culturally more controversial commitments such as those under WTO agreements on health and safety are more rigidly protected under a property rule (subject only to the temporary flexibilities offered in the DSU). Similarly, why protect specific

[79] Although the shift from GATT to WTO witnessed an increase in the number of reservations to renegotiate tariff concessions pursuant to GATT Article XXVIII:5, this increase in reservations or potential exit options did not result in more actual renegotiations taking place. On the contrary, during the period 1995–9 the lowest number of tariff renegotiations actually took place (eight as opposed to, for example, fifty-six in the period 1980–9). See Anwarul Hoda, *Tariff Negotiations and Renegotiations under the GATT and the WTO: Procedures and Practices* (Cambridge: Cambridge University Press, 2001), at 88–89 and 107. Similarly, since its creation in 1995, GATS Article XXI (renegotiation of specific commitments in trade in services) has so far only been invoked once (in the context of the *US – Gambling* dispute, discussed *supra*, chapter 4 note 13).

[80] See *supra*, chapter 4 note 13.

commitments under GATS under a liability rule (GATS Article XXI) and all other GATS commitments (such as those on domestic regulation under GATS Article VI, which are often more controversial) more rigidly under the property rule of the DSU?

(c) *Investor protection under NAFTA and BITs*

Another example of liability protection under current international law is investor protection under NAFTA Chapter 11 and most bilateral investment treaties (BITs). When it comes to expropriation by governments of foreign investments or investors the entitlement is clearly protected by a liability rule: non-discriminatory expropriations for a public purpose are not even breach of treaty for as long as full compensation is paid.[81] In other words, governments can expropriate for as long as they "pay for it." Other entitlements have similar, though less outspoken, liability features: a violation of national treatment or fair and equitable treatment, for example, does violate the treaty, but the remedy for it is explicitly limited to compensation, not restitution or specific performance.[82] As a result, states cannot be forced to, for example, withdraw a discriminatory

[81] Article 1110, North American Free Trade Agreement, 17 December 1992, entry into force 1 January 1994, 32 ILM 289 (NAFTA).

[82] Article 1134.1, NAFTA: "Where a Tribunal makes a final award against a Party, the Tribunal may award only: (a) monetary damages, and any applicable interest; or (b) restitution of property, in which case the award shall provide that the disputing Party may pay monetary damages, and any applicable interest, in lieu of restitution."

environmental statute or award a contract to an unfairly treated foreign investor. The only remedy that investors can expect is, instead, compensation. Although this surely means that such entitlements under investment treaties (compensation only) are less protected than those under trade agreements (where normally specific performance is required), in chapter 6 below (and as hinted at earlier) it will, however, be explained that the mere fact that back-up enforcement (step 3) is limited to compensation or 1:1 retaliation does not necessarily imply that the level of protection is that of a liability rule. One of the core arguments of this book is that step 2 and step 3 must be distinguished and that it is inappropriate to engage in reverse-engineering, i.e., to decide on the level of protection under step 2 based solely on the formal remedies in step 3.

The liability-type scheme thus imposed in investment treaties can be explained within the framework of this book. It was made possible largely because NAFTA Chapter 11 includes a compulsory investor–state dispute settlement system which offers collective valuation. As the entitlement protected centers on physical investments of money in a foreign country, that is, goods that are relatively fungible (rather than unique), the cost of errors in collective valuation are likely to be lower. Importantly, the problem of collecting and distributing compensation was also dealt with. Investors have private standing and therefore directly receive money compensation. In other words, even when piercing the state veil, unilateral takings with full compensation are likely to be Pareto superior as the actual investor-victim gets compensated directly. Moreover, the system is supported by efficient back-up enforcement, namely domestic courts which have an obligation to recognize and enforce NAFTA Chapter 11 awards. A similar mechanism is at work for investor–state arbitration awards under the World Bank's ICSID Convention.[83]

[83] ICSID tribunals are unlikely to award specific performance and, instead, remain focused on compensation. To that extent, they offer liability, not property, protection. Yet, such liability protection was made possible because of a strong dispute settlement mechanism including, specifically, automatic enforcement before domestic courts of any money awards. See Article 54.1, Convention for the Settlement of Investment Disputes between States and Nationals of Other States, 18 March 1965, entry into force 14 October 1966, 575 UNTS 159 (ICSID Convention): "Each Contracting State shall recognize an award rendered pursuant to this Convention as binding and enforce the *pecuniary* obligations imposed by that award within its territories as if it were a final judgment of a court in that State" (emphasis added).

6

Back-up enforcement in international law

As pointed out in chapter 3, how and how strongly entitlements are protected – either as inalienable or by a property rule or a liability rule – must be distinguished from what the system does in case the rules of protection are not respected, that is, when faced with extra-contractual behavior (back-up enforcement). Earlier, I referred to this distinction as one between second- and third-order questions. I also pointed out that whilst in domestic law back-up enforcement is a given (there are police, bailiffs and prisons) in international law (which generally lacks central enforcement) the third-order question of back-up enforcement becomes a crucial part of the equation. As a result, even though this book focuses on the second-order question of how international law ought to protect entitlements, as noted earlier, any such inquiry must be made in the context of the third step of back-up enforcement.

Logically, one would expect that higher levels of protection will also be backed up with higher or stronger remedies in case that level is not met. Put differently, the more ambitious the goal, the more forceful the instruments to achieve that goal. This is exactly what we see in domestic law. Where entitlements are (highly) protected as inalienable (such as in criminal law) back-up enforcement takes the form of imprisonment, sometimes even the death penalty. The next level of protection by property rule is, in turn, backed up with court injunctions and fines, coupled, if necessary, with imprisonment. Both go well beyond mere compensation and add what Calabresi and Melamed have called a "kicker" which, in the example of property rules, "represents society's need to keep all property rules from being changed at will into liability rules."[1] Finally, in case someone takes an entitlement protected by a liability rule without paying compensation, the holder of the entitlement can ask a court to objectively value the required level of compensation and, subsequently, enforce payment, if necessary with the help of bailiffs.

In international law, however, the situation is strikingly different, as we are faced with what is, at first sight, a double paradox. First, although international law, by default, ambitiously protects entitlements as property, back-up enforcement in case this rule of protection is not respected corresponds rather to what we would expect under a liability rule (compensation and proportional countermeasures). In other words, though more strongly protected as property, back-up enforcement in international law appears to be weaker. At first sight at least, international law does not seem to have Calabresi and Melamed's "kicker." Section 1 below explains, however, that international law has its own "kicker," not in the form of formal, legal remedies but in the form of what I will call "community costs." Although this "kicker" will, in many cases, be sufficient to back up property protection, its informal nature makes it difficult to predict and calibrate back-up enforcement in international law. Where

[1] Guido Calabresi and A. Douglas Melamed, "Property Rules, Liability Rules, and Inalienability: One View of the Cathedral" (1972), 85 *Harvard LR* 1,089, at 1,126.

international law is more developed and institutionalized we would, however, expect more variety and a sliding scale of back-up enforcement similar to domestic law. Second, and ultimately more worrisome, those entitlements that international law protects most strongly as inalienable (*jus cogens* and collective obligations) risk, paradoxically, benefiting only from the weakest form of back-up enforcement (Section 2). This paradox has led, and continues to lead, to demands for more effective alternatives to enforce *jus cogens* and collective obligations away from the state-to-state model.

1 The puzzle of property protection backed-up by "mere" compensation and proportional countermeasures

As described in chapter 5, whereas many entitlements in domestic law are protected by a mere liability rule, international entitlements are, by default, protected by a property rule. This rule requires, in principle, restitution and performance instead of only compensation. Given the inherent weakness of international law (in particular, the lack of centralized power) this may come as a surprise. In the face of weakness, is international law trying to be "more Catholic than the pope"? In chapter 4, I explained this apparent puzzle of an inherently weak system strongly protecting entitlements as property: it is largely *because of* – not despite – the weaknesses of international law that international entitlements are, by default, protected as property. More particularly, it is because of the absence and/or costs of a collective valuation mechanism that a liability rule under current international law is unlikely to work. These weaknesses of international law do *not stop*, or *prevent it*, from the relatively high level of property protection. Rather it is those weaknesses that partly *explain* the default rule of property protection. Conversely, it is in those areas of international law that are the most developed, normatively and institutionally, that we can expect liability instead of property protection, not the other way around.

Moving to the next step of back-up enforcement, a new puzzle arises. Though highly protected as property, in the event that the rules of property protection are flouted, international law offers only the type of back-up enforcement we would expect for liability protection. Indeed, in case the taker of an international entitlement protected as property fails to meet its obligation of restitution and/or specific performance (that is, cessation of ongoing breach), the back-up is merely (1) reparation for harm caused.[2] If the wrongdoer refuses to pay reparation, and to separately induce specific performance, the remedy of last resort is simply (2) *proportional* countermeasures,[3] that is, countermeasures

[2] Article 36.1, ILC Articles: "The State responsible for an internationally wrongful act is under an obligation to compensate for the damage caused thereby, insofar as such damage is not made good by restitution." More generally, Article 31.1 provides: "The responsible State is under an obligation to make full reparation for the injury caused by the internationally wrongful act."

[3] Article 49, ILC Articles: "An injured State may only take countermeasures against a State which is responsible for an internationally wrongful act in order to induce that State to comply with its obligations under Part Two," in particular, to induce cessation of the breach and payment of reparation.

"commensurate with the injury suffered, taking into account the gravity of the internationally wrongful act and the rights in question."[4] In case of material breach of treaty, one may add (3) suspension or termination of the treaty by the victim as against the wrongdoing state.[5] Crucially, at least under the default rules of general international law, genuine sanctions or punishment, in the form of either fines or punitive (even disproportional) countermeasures, are prohibited.[6]

[4] Article 51, ILC Articles. See also ILC Article 37.3, in respect of the remedy of "satisfaction" (available insofar as breach "cannot be made good by restitution or compensation" and which can take the form of "an acknowledgement of the breach, an expression of regret, a formal apology or another appropriate modality"): "Satisfaction shall not be out of proportion to the injury and may not take a form humiliating to the responsible State."

[5] Article 60, VCLT.

[6] The Commentary to ILC Article 51, at p. 344, notes: "a clearly disproportionate measure may well be judged not to have been necessary to induce the responsible State to comply with its obligations but to have had a punitive aim and to fall outside the purpose of countermeasures enunciated in article 49." In respect of compensation, the Commentary to ILC Article 36, at pp. 245–6, notes: "Compensation corresponds to the financially assessable damage suffered by the injured State or its nationals. It is not concerned to punish the responsible State, nor does compensation have an expressive or exemplary character." As concerns satisfaction, the Commentary to ILC Article 37, at p. 268, states: "satisfaction is not intended to be punitive in character, nor does it include punitive damages": Commentaries to the Draft Articles on the Responsibility of States for Internationally Wrongful Acts (2001), GAOR 56th Session, Supplement no. 10 (A/56/10). On punitive damages in international law, see N. Jørgensen, "A Reappraisal of Punitive Damages in International Law" (1997), 68 *BYBIL*, 247; S. Wittich, "Awe of the Gods and Fear of the Priests: Punitive Damages in the Law of State Responsibility" (1998), 3

In contrast, in domestic law, fines and/or punishment are exactly what we expect as back-up enforcement for property rules. To deter non-consensual takings of entitlements (such as my property entitlement to my house), fines are then set so as to exceed the expected gain from breach multiplied by the inverse of the probability of a fine being effectively imposed: if, for instance, the probability of detection and punishment is one out of five, the optimal fine is set at the expected gain multiplied by five.[7] For others, the optimal fine equals not the expected *gain* but the *harm* caused by breach multiplied by the inverse of the probability of being caught.[8] In general international law, however, no such calculation is made, as fines and punishment are by definition prohibited and only reparation and proportional countermeasures are allowed in response to breach.

In sum, international law sets for itself a level of protection that is *higher* than that for many domestic law norms (property versus liability protection). Yet, the instruments to achieve that higher level of protection (ultimately, reparation

Austrian R Int Eur L 31. Equally, based on DSU Article 22.4 (requiring "equivalence" between trade suspensions and the harm caused by the original breach), WTO arbitrators under DSU Article 22.6 have consistently rejected punitive suspensions (see, for example, *US – 1916 Act*, para. 5.22).

[7] See, for example, L. A. Bebchuk and L. Kaplow, "Optimal Sanctions and Differences in Individuals' Likelihood of Avoiding Detection" (1993), 13 *Int Rev L Econ* 217 and Wouter Wils, "Optimal Antitrust Fines: Theory and Practice" (2006), 29 *World Comp L Econ R* 183, at 190–1.

[8] Gary Becker, "Crime and Punishment: An Economic Approach" (1968), 76 *J Polit Econ* 169, and W. M. Landes, "Optimal Sanctions for Antitrust Violations" (1983), 50 *U Chicago LR* 652.

and proportional countermeasures) are *weaker* than those available in domestic law. How can one explain this puzzle?

European absolutists are likely to bow their heads to this puzzle and, in the same breath, argue for stronger back-up enforcement in international law, such as punitive sanctions.[9] Critics of international law, in contrast, including what I called American voluntarists, are likely to point at currently weak back-up enforcement to argue that, notwithstanding the stated goal of property protection, international entitlements are actually protected by a mere liability rule. On this view, as breach only results in compensation and proportional countermeasures, how can one claim that states must perform their commitments even if the cost of compliance outweighs the cost of defection? Put differently, with such weak back-up enforcement, how can one contest that international law permits efficient breach? From this perspective, the stated goal of property protection is, at best, overshooting: in the hope that more states will *actually* comply, international law raised the bar in its official *expectation* of how strictly states *ought to* comply. Knowing far too well that states cannot be forced into restitution or specific performance (there is no international

[9] See, for example, Petros Mavroidis, "Remedies in the WTO Legal System: Between a Rock and a Hard Place" (2000), 11 *EJIL* 763 (at 811, arguing that "for legal security to be served, *institutional* rather than individual grounds must be agreed and inserted in the contract that will guarantee respect at all times," and at 812, discussing punitive damages in the WTO). See also Benjamin Brimayer, "Bananas, Beef and Compliance in the WTO: The Inability of the WTO Dispute Settlement Process to Achieve Compliance from Superpower Nations" (2001), 10 *Minnesota J Global Trade* 133.

police), international law would then be imposing its high level of protection in the hope that states will at least be inclined to pay reparation. This would be like imposing a speed limit of 40 mph hoping that, since there is no real penalty linked to speeding anyhow, drivers will at least slow down to 60 mph. At worst, the stated goal of property protection is, for outright critics of international law, completely irrelevant: as states are purely self-interested and perform their commitments only for instrumental reasons, the only thing that counts is back-up enforcement. On this view, if breach is ultimately met only with compensation and proportional countermeasures, the second-order question of how entitlements are protected (and with it the bulk of this book) is irrelevant.

In the context of WTO law, for example, Joel Trachtman agrees that formally WTO entitlements are protected by a property rule, but submits that:

> a legal realist, and a legal economist, would ask not what the formal law specifies, but what it does in response to breach. *Ubi ius ibi remedium.* Here, the law in action clearly does not operate as a property rule. States that violate WTO law are not subject to enforceable specific performance-type remedies, nor do they experience any penalty for their violation beyond the potential authorization of withdrawal of equivalent concessions . . . So, as a matter of fact and practice, if not as a matter of legal doctrine, the WTO legal system is best characterized as employing a liability rule, rather than a property rule.[10]

[10] See Joel P. Trachtman, "Building the WTO Cathedral" (2006), available at http://ssrn.com/abstract=815844, at p. 23. See also at p. 21: "Indeed,

Going one step further, Schwartz and Sykes point at weak back-up enforcement (equivalent suspension of concessions) to argue, deductively, that even formally WTO entitlements are not protected by a property rule. If WTO members had preferred specific performance, their argument goes, they would have provided for sanctions that were more than equivalent to the harm caused. Since they did not do so, according to Schwartz and Sykes, WTO entitlements are formally and in practice protected by a mere liability rule.[11]

An alternative and better explanation for the puzzle at hand is, however, available. First, there are good reasons why international law avoids punitive sanctions (section (a) below). Although analogies with domestic law may urge traditional supporters of international law to solve the puzzle by merely strengthening formal remedies ("harder law is

if the goal were simply to induce compliance through the actions of government operatives, then penalties calculated to induce action by these operatives would be appropriate. But the goal is not necessarily to induce compliance in all cases. Rather, the goal seems to be to induce compliance when compliance is efficient, and breach when it is not."

[11] Warren Schwartz and Alan Sykes, "The Economic Structure of Renegotiation and Dispute Resolution in the World Trade Organization" (2002), 31 *J Leg Stud* 179, at 191 ("If WTO members really wanted to make compliance with dispute resolution findings mandatory, they would have imposed some greater penalty for noncompliance to induce it"), and Alan Sykes, "The Remedy for Breach of Obligations under the WTO Dispute Settlement Understanding: Damages or Specific Performance?" in Marco Bronckers and Reinhard Quick (eds.), *New Directions in International Economic Law: Essays in Honour of John H. Jackson* (New York: Springer, 2000), 349. See also David J. Bederman, "Counterintuiting Countermeasures" (2002), 96 *AJIL* 817, at 818.

better law"), this tendency must, therefore, be tempered. Second, even with the relatively weak back-up enforcement of compensation and proportional countermeasures in hand (hereafter referred to as 1:1 retaliation), the stated goal of property protection can and usually is met through informal remedies, in particular the "kicker" of what I will call "community costs" (sections (b) and section (c)). In addition, the hidden force of even the formal remedy of 1:1 retaliation should not be underestimated (section (d)). As a result, the current combination of formal and informal instruments of back-up enforcement in international law does not, generally speaking, undermine the default goal of property protection, let alone the usefulness of distinguishing levels of protection from back-up enforcement. Yet, since especially informal remedies (such as community costs) are difficult to measure, whether current back-up enforcement of international law is optimal is another question. What one would expect, however, is that where international law is more developed and institutionalized, a richer variety and possibly a sliding scale of back-up enforcement similar to domestic law will emerge.

(a) Good reasons to limit countermeasures to 1:1 retaliation

Descriptively, the fact that international law prohibits punitive sanctions – i.e., offers a relatively weak instrument of back-up enforcement, namely 1:1 retaliation – is easily explained: first, because of the consensual nature of international law and its status of a largely incomplete contract; second, because of the lack of centralized control over breach; third, due to power imbalances between states.

First, states, including the most powerful ones, are hesitant to enter a regime with strict remedies and tough punishments. Knowing that they may end up not only as complainants but also as defendants, states want to maintain some wiggle room.[12] Such flexibility may be sought after as an exit option to openly violate the agreement in case, for example, political or economic circumstances change or, more likely, so as not to be punished for good-faith implementation which turns out to constitute breach.[13] As noted earlier, treaties are incomplete contracts that cannot foresee all situations. They are also increasingly vague, especially when multilaterally negotiated, so that states acting in good faith may subsequently be found to violate the agreement.

[12] George Downs and David Rocke, *Optimal Imperfection: Domestic Uncertainty and Institutions in International Relations* (Princeton: Princeton University Press, 1995). As Robert Hudec noted in the context of the GATT/WTO: "The optimum legal system is not simply the strongest legal system. It is the legal system that will be most helpful in enforcing one's trade agreement rights as complainant, while at the same time preserving the desired degree of freedom to deal with adverse legal rulings against one's own behavior": Robert Hudec, "Broadening the Scope of Remedies in WTO Dispute Settlement," in Friedl Weiss and Jochem Wiers (eds.), *Improving WTO Dispute Settlement Procedures* (London: Cameron May Publishers, 2000), 345, at 350.

[13] As one WTO arbitrator noted: "In WTO dispute settlement cases, it is probably true that most defending parties argue in good faith that they believed the measures at issue were in conformity with the relevant provisions of the WTO Agreement" (*Canada – Aircraft Credits and Guarantees*, Arbitration under Article 22.6 of the DSU, para. 399).

As a result, if international law were to impose a back-up enforcement mechanism that is too forceful, it might either deter participation in what is essentially a consent-based system or, for those who did join but now face harsh penalties, may lead to exit from the treaty.[14] In domestic law, neither the front-end concern of attracting participation nor the back-end concern of avoiding exit plays a role: a domestic legislator rules by fiat and citizens cannot exit from specific rules (other than through emigration and/or denouncing citizenship). This makes it much easier, and more appropriate, for domestic law to have strict back-up enforcement as compared to international law. As David Palmeter points out in response to claims that current WTO remedies are too weak (no retroactive damages and even prospectively only equivalent retaliation is offered): "It is important to understand ... that the remedy that exists in the WTO is the remedy that Member governments found they were willing to accept as successful claimants – no doubt because they were unwilling to commit themselves to providing more as unsuccessful defendants."[15]

[14] As Anne-Marie Slaughter noted: "Forcing a situation in which a losing litigant is automatically forced to comply with the panel judgment ... is bound to make some States law-breakers": Anne-Marie Slaughter, "International Law and International Relations" (2000), 285 *Recueil des Cours* 9, at 165.

[15] David Palmeter, "The WTO Dispute Settlement System in the Next Ten Years," Presentation at Columbia University Conference on *The WTO at 10: Governance, Dispute Settlement and Developing Countries*, 7 April, 2006, available at www.sipa.columbia.edu/wto/pdfs/PalmeterWorkingPaper.pdf.

Along similar lines, Scott and Stephan refer to sociological studies[16] to demonstrate that formal enforcement and material sanctions may even crowd out or diminish the effectiveness of informal incentives that motivate compliance, in particular, the instinct to reciprocate.[17]

Second, limiting countermeasures to 1:1 retaliation in a decentralized legal system introduces a stabilizing constraint and minimizes the overall cost of breach and deterrence. Domestic legal systems went through a similar process. Francesco Parisi describes how, in ancient law, remedies evolved from discretionary retaliation (that is, unregulated retaliation imposing punishment much more severe than the harm done, e.g., sevenfold retaliation[18]) to a system of proportional retaliation or the biblical *lex talionis* ("an eye for an eye,"[19] setting a limit of 1:1 as the maximum

[16] In particular, Stewart Macaulay, "Non-Contractual Relations in Business" (1963), 28 *Am Soc R* 555. Macaulay's subjects reported that legal sanctions were not only unnecessary but might well have undesirable effects, as the invocation of legal enforcement might be seen as a betrayal of trust or an instinct to engage in sharp practice.

[17] Robert Scott and Paul Stephan, *The Limits of Leviathan* (Cambridge: Cambridge University Press, 2006), 35, at 44. On that basis, they suggest that "the hardening of . . . obligations through formal, third-party enforcement may deny states the opportunity to demonstrate that they have the capacity and desire to cooperate, and in effect restricts cooperation to those subjects where independent observers can verify the conditions for cooperation and sanction defections. In this way, formal enforcement can impede rather than promote valuable cooperation" (at 37).

[18] See Gen. 4:15, 4:23–4 and Prov. 6:13.

[19] See Exod. 21:23–4 and Lev. 24:17–22.

penalty for a crime).[20] Even though in a system of sevenfold retaliation no rational breach would be expected (the cost of breach is simply too high), the reality was that involuntary disturbance of the original peaceful equilibrium did occur and, if misperceived by at least one group, triggered very costly feuds. In the following passage the analogy to international law is readily made:

> In the absence of fixed rules [i.e., 1:1 retaliation], the magnitude of the victim's retaliation was often exacerbated by the victim's partisan bias, leading clans to overestimate the gravity of their harm and to retaliate in excess of the original loss. In turn, the clan suffering an excessive retaliation often felt entitled to respond with the infliction of new harm to the other party. This regime of retaliatory threats risked degenerating into spirals of escalating violence.[21]

Proportional countermeasures in international law can, therefore, be seen as a coordination mechanism to reduce the risk of escalating violence and retaliation, that is, a system of predictable and non-discretionary retaliation that promotes stability and overall efficiency.[22] As Robert Axelrod

[20] Francesco Parisi, "The Genesis of Liability in Ancient Law" (2001), 3 *Am L Econ R* 82. See also Elisabeth Zoller, *Unilateral Peacetime Remedies: An Analysis of Countermeasures* (Dobbs Ferry: Transnational Publishers, 1984), at 14 (observing that "in primitive societies, reciprocity is the central principle of life").

[21] Parisi, "The Genesis of Liability in Ancient Law," at 87.

[22] See Edith Hamilton, *The Greek Way* (New York: W. W. Norton, 1993). See also *Case Concerning the Air Services Agreement of 27 March 1946 between the United States of America and France*, 18 UNRIAA 417, at 445,

has argued, in environments characterized by the absence of hierarchy, tit-for-tat (or more precisely nine-tenths of a tit for a tat) is the best strategy for inducing cooperation among egotistical actors.[23] Interestingly, as is largely the case in current international law,[24] this 1:1 limit in ancient law was generally applicable and independent of the level of social undesirability of the crime and the probability of detection of the wrongdoer.[25]

Third, the imbalance of power between states offers an additional reason to opt for proportional instead of punitive countermeasures. When it comes to back-up enforcement, weaker states are, indeed, in a particularly difficult predicament. On the one hand, they want stronger remedies and treaties with real teeth; if not, powerful states may not comply. On the other hand, weak states have historically faced "gunboat diplomacy" and over-enforcement by powerful states. As a result, they are the first ones to benefit from limits on the legality of countermeasures and the requirement that

para. 91: "It goes without saying that recourse to counter-measures involves the great risk of giving rise, in turn, to a further reaction, thereby causing an escalation which will lead to a worsening of the conflict. Counter-measures therefore should be a wager on the wisdom, not on the weakness of the other Party. They should be used with a spirit of great moderation and be accompanied by a genuine effort at resolving the dispute."

[23] Robert Axelrod, *The Evolution of Cooperation* (New York: Basic Books, 1985), 136–9.

[24] But see the special rules for *jus cogens*, discussed *infra* text at note 72, and also ILC Article 51, which permits "taking into account the gravity of the internationally wrongful act and the rights in question."

[25] Parisi, "The Genesis of Liability in Ancient Law," at 85.

countermeasures be proportional. In that sense, the law on countermeasures is as much about limiting excessive self-help and leveling the playing field between hugely unequal players, as it is about effectively inducing compliance. As Schwartz and Sykes pointed out in the context of the WTO, the introduction of automatically and collectively authorized retaliation in the new WTO dispute settlement system was in response "not so much to the undercompliance with substantive obligations that arises absent these sanctions, but to the danger of excessive unilateral sanctions that exists in the absence of centralized oversight regarding the magnitude of sanctions."[26]

(b) How 1:1 retaliation can achieve property protection: the "kicker" of community costs

Explaining why international law limits countermeasures to 1:1 retaliation is one thing and relatively easy. It does not contradict American voluntarism, or proponents of the idea that international entitlements are in practice,[27] or even formally,[28] protected by a mere liability rule. Quite another thing is to demonstrate that mere compensation and proportional countermeasures can actually be sufficient as back-up enforcement for a property rule. If this book can demonstrate this latter point, my claim in favor of a default

[26] Schwartz and Sykes, "The Economic Structure of Renegotiation and Dispute Resolution in the WTO," at 204.

[27] Trachtman, "Building the WTO Cathedral."

[28] Alan Sykes, "The Economics of Public International Law," John M. Olin Law and Economics Working Paper No. 216, July 2004.

rule of property protection for international entitlements stands not only as a formal or prescriptive matter (second-order question) but also as a matter of law in action (third-order question), even in current international law.

As an empirical matter, we know that international cooperation is ubiquitous and that most international law is complied with most of the time.[29] In the WTO, for example, after ten years of operation and more than 350 disputes, in only a handful of cases did violators fail to perform and each of those cases pitted the US against the EC (not a small developing country against a powerful nation that could be unmoved by the threat of mere tit-for-tat retaliation). Knowing that back-up enforcement is limited to compensation and proportional countermeasures and, in the WTO, does not even include damages but only equivalent retaliation, how can this remarkable success rate be explained?[30]

[29] Louis Henkin, *How Nations Behave: Law and Foreign Policy*, 2nd edn (New York: Columbia University Press, 1979), 47; Robert Keohane, "International Relations and International Law: Two Optics" (1997), 38 *Harvard Int LJ* 487 ("Governments make a very large number of legal agreements, and, on the whole, their compliance with these agreements seems quite high. Yet what this level of compliance implies about the causal impact of commitments remains a mystery"); and Detlev Vagts, "The United States and Its Treaties: Observance and Breach" (2001), 95 *AJIL* 313, at 313 (arguing that "the U.S. record [regarding treaty observance] has not been as negative as some have feared but that anxieties have been needlessly fueled in recent years by the reckless language of both officials and scholars").

[30] One study, for example, concludes that the level of compliance with subsidy rules under the WTO agreement is higher than the level of compliance with German domestic rules on subsidization. See Michael Zurn and Jurgen Neyer, "Conclusions – The Conditions

With all the talk of promoting efficient breach, how come that so little of it materialized?[31] Similarly, the compliance rate with rules and judgments under the European Convention of Human Rights is stellar. Yet, the formal remedy of last resort offered by the European Court of Human Rights is mere money damages or "just satisfaction."[32] Does this, in effect, mean that human rights under the Convention are protected by a simple liability rule?

Two strands of arguments support the idea that compensation and proportional countermeasures or 1:1 retaliation can be sufficient to back up a property rule. First, and most importantly, states have incentives to perform their commitments besides formal sanctions or 1:1 retaliation, such as reputation costs, fear of emulation, community pressure, the normative pull of ideas and values and/or an urge to protect a particular institution or the international legal system more generally (hereafter referred to collectively as community costs). As one popular source put it, "[t]here are three basic flavors of incentive: economic, social, and moral. Very often a single incentive scheme will include all three varieties."[33] Secondly, and discussed in section (d), even 1:1

of Compliance," in Michael Zurn and Christian Joerges (eds.), *Law and Governance in Postnational Europe: Compliance beyond the Nation-State* (Cambridge: Cambridge University Press, 2005), at 183.

[31] See the sparse invocation of GATT/WTO liability mechanisms discussed *supra*, chapter 5 note 79.

[32] See *supra*, chapter 5 note 40.

[33] Steven Levitt and Stephen Dubner, *Freakonomics: A Rogue Economist Explores the Hidden Side of Everything* (New York: William Morrow, 2005), at 21.

retaliation itself is more forceful than one would think at first sight.

To begin with, 1:1 retaliation or formal sanctions are not the only costs of breach. Even if one assumes that states care only about their own interests and comply with international law for purely instrumental reasons, breach, in various degrees, also triggers reputation costs, fear of emulation and community pressure.[34] International affairs are a repeat game, in a variety of fields. Given the limited number of states, the impossibility of anonymity and the durability of state identities, reputation is a factor that matters.[35] As Andrew Guzman explains, "[a] reputation for compliance with international law is valuable because it allows states to make more credible promises to other states. This allows the state to extract greater concessions when it negotiates an international agreement."[36] The importance of reputation costs is far from unique to inter-state relations and cannot, therefore, be lightly rejected as a desperate attempt by international law supporters to give normative or instrumental value to international obligations. Under domestic law as well,

[34] Andrew Guzman, "International Law: A Compliance Based Theory" (2002), 90 *California LR* 1,823. See also George Norman and Joel P. Trachtman, "The Customary International Law Game" (2005), 99 *AJIL* 541; Edward T. Swaine, "Rational Custom" (2002), 52 *Duke LJ* 599; and long before, Robert O. Keohane, *After Hegemony: Cooperation and Discord in the World Political Economy* (Princeton: Princeton University Press, 1984).

[35] Robert Scott and Paul Stephan, *The Limits of Leviathan* (Cambridge: Cambridge University Press, 2006), at 121.

[36] Andrew Guzman, "Reputation and International Law" (2005), 34 *Georgia J Int Comp L* 379, at 383.

trust and reputation is one of the core ingredients of the rule of law and market capitalism. As Alan Greenspan – hardly an idealistic defender of law for the sake of law – put it:

> In a market system based on trust, reputation will have a significant economic value. Reputation, capitalized formally as "goodwill" on business balance sheets or otherwise, is an important contributor to the market value of a company. Reputation and the trust it fosters have always appeared to me to be the core required attributes of market capitalism. Laws [and the formal sanctions they impose] at best can prescribe only a small fraction of the day-by-day activities in the marketplace. When trust is lost, a nation's ability to transact business is palpably undermined.[37]

As a result, reputation encourages states to comply with international law, even where formal sanctions alone may not provide a sufficient incentive. Reputation can, in other words, help to explain why 1:1 retaliation can and, most often, does achieve property protection.

Fear of emulation, that is, realization that if I breach my obligation now, you may be less inclined to perform your obligations in the future, can play a similar role. In this context, Scott and Stephan refer to moralistic reciprocity or reciprocal fairness, linked to broader community pressure, as a potent additional means of self-enforcement besides retaliatory threats and reputational sanctions.[38] Moreover,

[37] Greenspan, *The Age of Turbulence* (New York: Penguin, 2007), at 256.

[38] Scott and Stephan, *The Limits of Leviathan*, at 154. They invoke, in particular, an empirical study by Ernst Fehr and Klaus Schmidt – "A

community pressure need not come from the outside or other states alone. An unequivocal, public condemnation of a state can mobilize domestic actors in that state to put pressure on the state to comply (be it consumers or domestic industries suffering from WTO breach or NGOs advocating human rights in case of human rights violations).

This is not to say that these "community costs" will always be sufficient or that they will always trigger significant or the same costs. Indeed, states can, for example, have multiple reputations (say, one in the field of trade, another for environmental compliance) and multiple reputational concerns (sometimes creating a reputation of toughness, including through violating the law) may be beneficial. Reputation may also attach more to regimes or governments than states, and as regimes change with some frequency, reputation costs may at times be perceived as less important.[39] Similarly, community pressure and the normative pull of ideas, values and the urge

Theory of Fairness, Competition and Cooperation" (1999), 114 *QJ Econ* 817 – that develops a theory of inequity aversion, combining features of both altruism and envy. Scott and Stephan distinguish simple reciprocity from moralistic reciprocity: "In the simple form of reciprocity, punishment for defection takes the form of withdrawal of future cooperation (e.g., if you cheat, I will not deal with you anymore). Moralistic reciprocity refers to more elaborate forms of punishment, including social ostracism, reduced status, fewer friends and fewer mating opportunities. Evolutionary theorists argue that simple reciprocity cannot support large scale human cooperation . . . But moralistic reciprocity offers a more plausible basis for establishing large scale patterns of cooperation because it provides many more ways that cooperators can punish defectors" (at 155).

[39] *Ibid.*, at 121.

to preserve international regimes may be stronger under, for example, the European Convention of Human Rights than under the UN Convention against Corruption. What reputation, fear of emulation and community pressure do achieve, however, is that they act at the margin, like all influences on state behavior, and in many cases help explain why even the most powerful states comply with international law even where the threat of proportional countermeasures in and of itself means nothing to them. For example, reputation, fear of emulation and the desire to uphold the WTO as an institution which serves US interests largely explains why the United States implemented adverse WTO rulings obtained against it by developing countries such as Brazil and Venezuela (*US – Gasoline*) or, even more so, Costa Rica (*US – Underwear*).[40] As Robert Hudec explains in the context of GATT: "The ultimate 'remedy' which made the GATT dispute settlement procedure as successful as it was [was] the force of community pressure. Community pressure is something that can be generated without an elaborate structure of remedial procedures."[41]

[40] See Schwartz and Sykes, "The Economic Structure of Renegotiation and Dispute Resolution in the WTO," at 196–7; Trachtman, "Building the WTO Cathedral," at 18 ("Reputation may help to explain why we observe widespread compliance with WTO law despite existing prospective-only remedies that would seem, considered alone, to provide incentives for breach"); Shannon K. Mitchell, "GATT, Dispute Settlement and Cooperation: A Note" (1997), 9 *Econ Polit* 97; Dan Kovenock and Marie Thursby, "GATT, Dispute Settlement and Cooperation" (1992), 4 *Econ Polit* 151.

[41] Hudec, "Broadening the Scope of Remedies in WTO Dispute Settlement," at 376.

Finally, if one is willing to go beyond purely instrumental reasons for why states comply with international law (an assumption we have stuck to so far), empirical evidence on individual behavior may further explain why states comply notwithstanding weak back-up enforcement.[42] Such other research includes, for example, that of Tom Tyler, whose psychological studies suggest that people comply with law because of procedural justice and ideas of fairness, that is, based on social relationships and ethical judgments, rather than purely instrumental reasons (e.g., the threat of formal sanctions or punishment).[43] If correct in the international context, compliance with international law would then at least partly be self-regulatory and Tyler's non-instrumental explanations could explain why states comply with international law even where the sanction for breach is "only" 1:1 retaliation. It is, indeed, not too speculative to imagine that

[42] If proponents of a pure rational choice approach to international law are allowed to apply to states rational actor models usually applied to individuals, we must be ready also to learn from other behavioral and sociological research on individual action and consider application of it to state action.

[43] Tom Tyler, *Why People Obey the Law* (Princeton: Princeton University Press, 2006). See also Colin Diver, "A Theory of Regulatory Enforcement" (1980), 28 *Pub Pol* 257, at 297 ("Businesses obey regulations for a host of reasons, moral or intellectual commitment to underlying regulatory objectives, belief in the fairness of the procedures that produced the regulations, pressure from peers, competitors, customers, or employees, conformity with a law-abiding self-image – in addition to fear of detection and punishment. It is a common place that no regulatory command will succeed without substantial voluntary compliance").

when, for example, US President George W. Bush considers foreign policy, he not only acts pursuant to an economic cost-benefit analysis, but is driven also by ideas (such as freedom) and moral principles (including religion). Following a different track, in an empirical study of neighborly relations between cattlemen in Shasta County, California, Robert Ellickson demonstrates that people frequently resolve their disputes in cooperative fashion without paying any attention to the laws that apply to those disputes.[44] Ellickson criticizes what he calls the legal centralism of law and economics theory which, like Thomas Hobbes, seems to deny the possibility that controllers other than the state or some centralized Leviathan could generate or protect entitlements.[45] If correct in the international context, what Ellickson refers to as "decentralized social forces" (including notice, gossip and the threat of force) contribute importantly to social order and may explain why, notwithstanding "mere" 1:1 retaliation, high levels of property protection can and are being achieved.

[44] Robert Ellickson, *Order without Law: How Neighbors Settle Disputes* (Cambridge, Mass.: Harvard University Press, 1991).

[45] *Ibid.*, at 138–9. Ellickson points, for example, to the fact that a few virtuous leaders at the highest level of social control create incentives for cooperative activity that cascade down. Such a critical mass of self-disciplined elders may, in his view, be as good a controller as Hobbes' Leviathan. This may explain why, in international law, cooperative behavior by mayor players such as the United States can be an important stimulus for cooperation.

(c) Community costs in a property regime as opposed to a liability regime

Obviously, community costs may induce compliance with both property and liability protection: under a liability rule, reputation may induce states to pay full compensation; under a property rule, reputation may convince states to perform their commitment. Yet, even if formal back-up enforcement under both regimes may be similar – as is apparently the case in international law, where the default property rule is backed up with "mere" compensation and 1:1 retaliation – the informal factor of community costs operates very differently. Under a property rule, community costs are, in essence, the "kicker" that achieves property protection.

Under a liability rule, the payment of compensation (as where a NAFTA party expropriates property but pays full compensation for it), or suffering of 1:1 retaliation (following, for example, unilateral tariff hikes or safeguards under GATT Articles XXVIII and XIX), is the end of the story and stops most, if not all, community costs. Indeed, as the state has then fully complied with its obligations under the liability rule by paying compensation, the state becomes a law-abider. Under a liability rule, compensation is merely the "price" for doing what is permitted and, with its payment, no breach and, hence, no community costs are triggered. Put differently, under a liability rule, compensation is part of the *intra*-contractual rules of step 2 (protection of entitlements), not of the *extra*-contractual sanctions of step 3 (back-up enforcement).

Under a property rule, in contrast, the payment of compensation or suffering of 1:1 retaliation (in, for example,

WTO dispute settlement), even where it is the only formal back-up, is nothing but a temporary solution and not the end of the story. As the ultimate goal is and remains performance (or consensual renegotiation of the commitment), the clock of community costs keeps ticking.[46] Under a property rule, rather than the "price" for doing what is permitted, compensation or 1:1 retaliation is a "sanction" for doing what is forbidden.[47] As a result, notwithstanding the payment of compensation or suffering of 1:1 retaliation, breach and with it community costs keep ticking. As Daniel Friedman pointed out in the domestic law context, the similarity in the end result – domestically, a money award; internationally, compensation and/or 1:1 retaliation – should not blur the fundamental distinction between the two situations. Under a liability rule (Friedman mentions eminent domain in public law; we could mention expropriation under NAFTA or tariff renegotiations and safeguards in the

[46] In the WTO context, for example, even after retaliation has been approved, the question of non-implementation by the original wrongdoer remains on the agenda of each and every session of the WTO's Dispute Settlement Body (DSB), "until the issue is resolved" (DSU, Article 21.6, also see *supra*, chapter 5 note 75). In other words, at each and every session of the DSB the wrongdoer is put on the spot and reminded by all other WTO members that performance is still lacking. This creates community costs even after retaliation has been approved.

[47] See Robert Cooter, "Prices and Sanctions" (1984), 84 *Columbia LR* 1,523, and J. C. Coffee, "Paradigms Lost: The Blurring of the Criminal and Civil Law Models – and What Can Be Done About It" (1992), 101 *Yale LJ* 1,875. That trade retaliation under the DSU is currently seen as a sanction rather than simply rebalancing the scales or compensation, see Steve Charnovitz, "Rethinking WTO Trade Sanctions" (2001), 94 *AJIL* 792.

WTO), the appropriation is lawful and permissible and the remedy of compensation is a perfect substitute for the right. In other words, it is the intra-contractual price to be paid for the entitlement. Under a property rule, in contrast (Friedman mentions the case in which conduct is wrongful but the remedy of the innocent party is limited to damages; we could mention a WTO-inconsistent trade restriction triggering 1:1 retaliation under the DSU or money damages before the European Court of Human Rights), the appropriation is not lawful, or permissible, and the remedy of compensation and/or retaliation is a sanction to vindicate the right, not a price to replace it.[48] In other words, it is the extra-contractual sanction to protect the entitlement (or to induce compliance), not the price for its lawful transfer. As Richard Brooks put it more recently, "[t]he power to perform or pay is not the same as the right to perform or pay."[49]

This fundamental distinction, notwithstanding the similarity in back-up enforcement, means that in a property regime, even after compensation and 1:1 retaliation, community costs keep running. This is not the case under a liability rule. Community costs can, therefore, be the "kicker" that ensures property protection. In Calabresi and Melamed's

[48] Daniel Friedmann, "The Efficient Breach Fallacy" (1989), 18 *J Leg Stud* 1, at 1 and 15–16. Using the example of nuisance, Friedman submits that the defendant had no right beforehand to pollute, although, *ex post facto*, the court confined the remedy to damages. Crucially, however, the limitation on the remedy does not amount to a license to commit a tort.

[49] Richard Brooks, "The Efficient Performance Hypothesis" (2006), 116 *Yale LJ* 568, at 572.

words, community costs are then what "keep[s] all property rules from being changed at will into liability rules."

Crucially, to trigger community costs, what matters is the existence of an obligation in the eyes of other states (say, other WTO members when it comes to a US breach) rather than a sense of legal obligation felt by the breaching state itself (*in casu*, the United States).[50] Put differently, if community costs are the "kicker" that back up property protection in international law, activation of this kicker turns on a clear community sense of there being an obligation of performance (rather than mere compensation).[51] As a result, and this is an important point, the second-order question of setting an agreed level of protection of entitlements is crucial – it sets the trigger and the level of community costs – even in the less developed system of international law. Unlike what American voluntarists may claim, the triple distinction introduced in this book – allocation, protection and back-up enforcement – does therefore matter, as it is the agreed level of protection that sets the trigger for, and determines the degree of, community costs and it is these community costs that, in many cases, tip the balance in favor of compliance.

In the WTO context, for example, this highlights the importance of the debate over whether WTO entitlements are

[50] See Andrew Guzman, "International Law: A Compliance Based Theory" (2002), 90 *California LR* 1823.

[51] In support, Trachtman, "Building the WTO Cathedral," at 37: "Reputational sanctions might still apply where a state fails to comply with the rules that can be understood as property rights, whereas if a rule is *understood* as a liability rule perhaps no reputational sanction would attach."

protected under a property or liability rule. If WTO members merely start *believing* that WTO entitlements are protected by a simple liability rule, this will reduce or may even take away the "kicker" of community costs, and with it the cost of breach. The debate on whether to introduce monetary compensation for WTO breach offers a good illustration.[52] If the WTO would mandate such compensation (especially as a replacement of, instead of in addition to, retaliation), it is crucially important to specify that this compensation is there to make up for damage (and possibly to induce compliance), not to replace actual performance. If not, compensation risks being regarded by the trade community as a substitute for compliance and the payment of compensation may stop community costs.[53] This, in turn, would seriously weaken

[52] For such proposal, see Communication by Ecuador, TN/DS/W9, at 6 ("compliance should be given more encouragement and, for this purpose, compensation could be an extremely useful tool"); Communication by the Group of Least Developing Countries, TN/DS/W/17, at 4 ("a strong case for monetary compensation can be made. This remedy is important for developing and least developed countries, and for any economy that suffers for the time that an offending measure remains in place"); and Marco Bronckers and Naboth van den Broek, "Financial Compensation in the WTO" (2005), 8 *JIEL* 101.

[53] For reactions along those lines see India's response to an EC proposal promoting compensation in the WTO: "In fact if the EC's proposal on making trade compensation more realistic is accepted, it could serve as an inducement for the losing party not to comply promptly with the DSB decision. If the EC agree that the key objective of the dispute settlement mechanism is to secure withdrawal of WTO inconsistent measures, how does the proposal for making trade compensation more realistic encourage this objective?" (Communication from India, Document TN/DS/W5, 7 May 2002). Also Chile's position expressed at

back-up enforcement (no more "kicker" of community costs) and could paradoxically mean that an additional instrument of back-up enforcement (monetary compensation) leads to less, rather than more, compliance. Eventually, this may undermine the property regime in the first place and replace it by a liability rule.[54]

Although examining a completely unrelated field, this is exactly what happened in a study of day-care centers in Israel.[55] Apparently, the mere rule that kids were supposed to be picked up at 4 p.m. did not prevent some parents from being late. To address this problem, the decision was made to fine any parent arriving late $3 per child for each incident. Now, what happened? Instead of down, the number of late pickups went up. How can this be explained? Not only was the fine too small but, more importantly, it substituted an economic incentive (the $3 penalty) for a moral/community incentive (the guilt and community pressure that parents were supposed to feel when they came late). As risks being the case in the WTO, monetary compensation, in effect,

a meeting of the DSB, WT/DSB/M/6, at 7 ("Chile was not particularly attracted to the proposals on compensation, as there was the tendency to see it as a substitute for compliance").

54 This is not to say that compensation in the WTO context is necessarily a bad idea, only to point out that it is important to put it in context. As in general international law, it may be better to combine compensation with retaliation as the two instruments serve distinct roles, the former an inducement for the wrongdoer to comply, the latter making up for damage caused to the victim.

55 Uri Gneezy and Aldo Rustichini, "A Fine Is a Price" (2000), 29 *J Leg Stud* 1.

changed a property regime (kids must be picked up at 4 p.m.) into a liability regime ($3 gets you off the hook).

Conversely, in NAFTA, where (unlike in the WTO) breach does not trigger an obligation of specific performance, the level of protection is determined not only by the formal remedy provided (mere compensation, reminiscent of liability protection), but also by the overall perception of how "bad" it is (e.g., for a country's overall investment climate and reputation) to breach NAFTA in the first place. If NAFTA parties, investors and society at large trigger community costs for breach alone, these community costs, combined with the formal remedy of compensation, may provide strong incentives to comply with NAFTA even where a purely economic cost-benefit analysis would call for breach (the benefits of, say, discriminating against the foreign investor outweigh the compensation to be paid). In the end, based largely on community perceptions, as much as WTO protection could shift from property to liability, NAFTA protection could, thereby, shift from liability to property.

(d) How 1:1 retaliation can achieve property protection: the hidden force of 1:1 retaliation itself

A second strand of arguments for why compensation and proportional countermeasures can achieve property protection relates to the fact that 1:1 retaliation itself is more forceful than one may think at first sight. It is crucially important to realize that retaliation in international law (with the notable exception of the WTO) is a remedy *in addition to* compensation and (in all cases, including the WTO) destined primarily to punish the wrongdoer, not to compensate the victim. When I take your eye in response to you taking my eye, I do not get my eye back; nor am I compensated in any way for previously losing my eye. In WTO law, however, the oft-repeated argument that trade retaliation is shooting oneself in the foot and therefore inappropriate as a remedy[56] overlooks this basic point: as much as me taking out your eye is costly for me as a victim, it is quite natural that higher tariffs as a form of retaliation can be costly also for the victim of WTO breach.[57] As Reto Malacrida phrased it recently, "[i]t is important ... not to lose sight of the fact that retaliation is about inducing compliance on the part of a recalcitrant responding Member. It other words, it is about law enforcement, and law enforcement invariably comes at an economic cost."[58]

In addition to being focused on causing pain to the wrongdoer (not compensating the victim), 1:1 retaliation is linked to the *loss* suffered by the victim, not the *benefit* derived by the wrongdoer. In other words, countermeasures must be proportional to the damage caused, not to the gain

[56] See Steve Charnovitz, "Rethinking WTO Trade Sanctions" (2001), 94 *AJIL* 792, who, on that and other grounds, suggests replacing trade retaliation with other types of sanctions.

[57] Recall, however, that unlike general international law WTO remedies do not include compensation for harm caused and offer only retaliation. This may explain why from the early GATT days there has been confusion as to the goal of trade retaliation, namely: is it compensatory or awarded to induce compliance, or both?

[58] Reto Malacrida, "Towards Sounder and Fairer WTO Retaliation" (2008), 42 *Journal of World Trade* 3, at 12.

obtained from breach. Unlike disgorgement (which takes away benefits from the violator), and like compensation, retaliation is linked to harm. In the WTO, for example, the level of trade retaliation is not set with reference to the gains made by the violator. Rather, retaliation must be equivalent to the nullification and impairment caused to the victim of the breach.[59] Now, as Parisi points out, "[u]nder usual circumstances, the wrongdoer derives a benefit that is less than the harm suffered by the victim."[60] If, for example, you take out my eye, I will most likely suffer more from losing my eye than you gain from taking it out. As a result, the pain I cause to you with 1:1 retaliation (calibrated as it is on *my* earlier *pain* of losing my eye) is likely to outweigh the benefit or gain that you obtained from originally taking my eye. Coming back to the WTO example, the expected benefits of a WTO-inconsistent trade restriction (if there are any benefits at all) are likely to be smaller than the harm caused to foreign trading nations, especially if more than one country (and potentially 15 other nations) are affected and must be compensated. In that scenario, the threat of 1:1 retaliation can be more than sufficient to back up property protection.

[59] Article 22.4, DSU. But note the case law on "appropriate countermeasures" under the WTO's subsidies agreement (Article 4.10). There, arbitrators have set the level of trade sanctions in response to so-called prohibited subsidies at an amount equal to the subsidy originally handed out. Thus, rather than focusing on the harm caused by the subsidy to other WTO members, arbitrators have centered on the benefit or gain bestowed on the subsidized industry in the wrongdoing country.

[60] Parisi, "The Genesis of Liability in Ancient Law," at 104.

Besides the fact that retaliation in international law comes in addition to compensation, and is focused on causing pain to the wrongdoer but calibrated on the harm done to the victim, the nature or type of 1:1 retaliation may also explain why it is, most often, sufficient to deter breach and to induce specific performance.[61] Unlike the biblical *lex talionis* ("an eye for an eye"), countermeasures in international law must not be of the same type as the original breach. Rather, the core limit is quantitative, not qualitative. In the WTO, for example, the victim of a WTO-inconsistent tariff on steel must not retaliate with an equivalent tariff on steel. Rather, the victim can suspend any trade concession of an equivalent value, be it tariffs on cars, oranges or textiles. This leeway as to the type of product or sector in which to retaliate has led to very effective retaliation, for example by the EC against US industries that were crucial in the Bush administration's 2004 re-election campaign. By thus mobilizing domestic US industries (*in casu*, Florida orange growers and North Carolina textile

[61] That states may breach but subsequently step in line in response to 1:1 retaliation can partly be explained by the fact that people, and therefore presumably governments, consistently tend to overestimate the probability of good things happening to them. See N. D. Weinstein, "Optimistic Biases about Personal Risks" (1989), 246 *Science* 1,232, and R. B Korobkin and T. S. Ulen, "Law and Behavioral Science: Removing the Rationality Assumption from Law and Economics" (2000), 88 *California LR* 1,051, at 1,091–5. Decision-makers are therefore likely to over-estimate, for example, the gains to be obtained from a WTO-inconsistent tariff. Once imposed, however, those gains may turn out to be lower, and although the *ex ante* expectation of gain may have exceeded the threat of 1:1 retaliation, *ex post* realization of gains may no longer do so. Hence, the tariff is withdrawn.

producers) against a WTO-inconsistent US steel tariff, 1:1 retaliation by the EC has, at least in political terms, proven to be more than a simple tit-for-tat. Combined with the already existing opposition against the steel tariff by US consumers of steel (e.g., the US car industry), the proposed EC retaliation, amongst other elements, led to the withdrawal of the tariff.[62] A similar process occurred in the *US – Foreign Sales Corporations* dispute. As Mark Movsesian remarks, without intruding directly on domestic institutions, "the genius of the retaliation remedy lies in its ability to use the domestic political process to achieve the public interest. By setting one collection of interest groups against another, the retaliation remedy encourages the adoption of free trade policies that benefit a nation's consumers as a whole."[63] In other words, under 1:1 retaliation, one is not limited as to the "hostage" one can take (e.g., the industry one will hit with higher tariffs); rather, one can and should be advised to take the hostage that "screams the loudest." Or as Malacrida put it in the WTO context, when it comes to retaliation, "compliance is to be

[62] See David Sanger, "A Blink from the Bush Administration," *NY Times*, 5 December 2003.

[63] Mark Movsesian, "Enforcement of WTO Rulings: An Interest Group Analysis" (2003), 32 *Hofstra LR* 1, at 4–5. Schwartz and Sykes ("The Economic Structure of Renegotiation and Dispute Resolution in the WTO," at 194) similarly refer to domestic costs of violation as a crucial engine that drives compliance with WTO law. Hudec, ("Broadening the Scope of Remedies in WTO Dispute Settlement"), in turn, warns that "[m]ore-than-equivalent retaliation would probably undermine the effort to enlist support for compliance within the target country. It would be perceived by the target country audience as taking unfair advantage of the violation" (at 23).

induced, not so much via the level of suspension of concessions or other obligations ... but through the selection of the concessions or other obligations to be suspended."[64]

Finally, although I have so far referred to countermeasures under general international law as 1:1 retaliation, there is some leeway to go above strict equivalence. First, proportionality is defined as a level "commensurate" with the injury suffered, instead of strict equivalence.[65] In case law, there has indeed been a tendency to accept countermeasures even though they exceeded exact equivalence for as long as they were not clearly disproportionate.[66] Second, recall that proportionality permits "taking into account the

[64] Malacrida, "Towards Sounder and Fairer WTO Retaliation," at 5.

[65] Recall, however, that in the WTO, DSU Article 22.4 does require "equivalence." At the same time, in respect of prohibited subsidies (Subsidies Agreement, Article 4.10), "appropriate countermeasures" are allowed which, in a footnote, is further specified as follows: "This expression is not meant to allow countermeasures that are disproportionate in light of the fact that the subsidies ... are prohibited." Also the original GATT Article XXIII:2 on trade suspensions refers to suspension "appropriate in the circumstances." See *supra*, chapter 5 note 76.

[66] See, for example, *Naulilaa (Responsibility of Germany for Damage Caused in the Portuguese Colonies in the South of Africa)*, 2 UNRIAA (1928), 1,013, at 1,028 ("one should certainly consider as excessive and therefore unlawful reprisals out of all proportion to the act motivating them") and *Case Concerning the Air Services Agreement of 27 March 1946 between the United States of America and France*, 18 UNRIAA (1978), 417, at 444, para. 83 (in that case there was no exact equivalence between France's refusal to allow a change of gauge in London on flights from the west coast of the United States and the United States' countermeasure which suspended Air France flights to Los Angeles altogether. The Tribunal nonetheless held the United States measures to be in conformity with the principle of

gravity of the internationally wrongful act and the rights in question." Hence, if the breach is particularly serious and/or the right protected particularly important, retaliation for a level higher than harm caused can be acceptable.[67] Both of these elements – proportional not equivalent; permission to take account of the gravity of breach and of rights – may further explain why proportional countermeasures can appropriately back up a property rule. Importantly, these elements also offer an entry way for international law to tailor back-up enforcement more precisely to the particular level of protection sought by each norm, as is casually done in domestic law.[68] One can, indeed, expect that where international law is more developed and institutionalized, a richer variety and possibly a sliding scale of back-up

proportionality because they "do not appear to be clearly disproportionate when compared to those taken by France").

67 For example, in *Gabčíkovo-Nagymaros Project (Hungary/Slovakia), ICJ Rep* 1997, p. 7, paras. 85 and 87 (citing *Territorial Jurisdiction of the International Commission of the River Oder*, PCIJ Series A no. 23 (1929), 27), the Court took into account the quality or character of the rights in question as a matter of principle and (like the Tribunal in the *Air Services* case, 18 UNRIAA 417) did not assess the question of proportionality only in quantitative terms.

68 Such tailoring, including a permission to go beyond mere equivalence, can already be seen in, for example, the case law on trade suspension under the WTO Subsidies Agreement. In *Canada – Aircraft Credits and Guarantees*, for example, Canada openly stated that it would not comply in respect of contracted but not yet delivered aircraft. On that ground, the arbitrators (in para. 3.121) decided to adjust the level upwards by 20 percent, i.e. "by an amount which we deem reasonably meaningful to cause Canada to reconsider its current position to maintain the subsidy at issue in breach of its obligations."

enforcement similar to domestic law will emerge. One such example is the Kyoto Protocol, where parties who exceed their emissions ceiling at the end of the implementation period will see the short-fall carried over to the next period. On top of that, and clearly as a form of punishment, an additional 30 percent can be added.[69] Yet, whenever treaty negotiators consider punitive remedies, they must take account of the reasons set out earlier (in section (a)) for why countermeasures in international law are normally limited to 1:1 retaliation (in particular, the need to attract participation and prevent exit in a consent-based system). In addition, negotiators must count for the community costs (discussed in sections (b) and (c)) when deciding on the optimal level of back-up enforcement and assessing whether punitive remedies are genuinely needed to achieve compliance.

2 The puzzle of *jus cogens* and collective obligations benefiting from the weakest form of back-up enforcement

In the previous section, I set out a first paradox of back-up enforcement in international law: though more

[69] Decision 24/CP.7 on Procedures and mechanisms relating to compliance under the Kyoto Protocol, FCCC/CP/2001/13/Add.3, Section XV.5(a): "Where the enforcement branch has determined that the emissions of a Party have exceeded its assigned amount . . . it shall declare that that party is not in compliance . . . and shall apply the following consequences: (a) Deduction from the Party's assigned amount for the second commitment period of a number of tones equal to 1.3 times the amount in tones of excess emissions."

strongly protected as property, back-up enforcement in international law appears to be weaker ("mere" compensation and proportional countermeasures). I subsequently explained this apparent paradox: first, there are good reasons for international law to avoid punitive sanctions; second, and crucially important, the "kicker" of non-legal remedies, in particular community costs, combined with the hidden force of 1:1 retaliation itself, can, and usually does, achieve the stated goal of property protection. As a result, the instruments of compensation and proportional countermeasures do not, generally speaking, undermine the default goal of property protection, let alone the usefulness of distinguishing levels of protection from back-up enforcement.

In addition, and more worrisome, a second paradox arises in respect of those entitlements which I described earlier as most strongly protected in international law, namely entitlements collectively held by the international community as a whole (*jus cogens*) or an entire group of states (collective obligations), referred to hereafter in combination as "community obligations." This second paradox can be summarized as follows: although *more strongly* protected as either super-inalienable (*jus cogens*) or prohibiting *inter se* transfers or contracting out (collective obligations), back-up enforcement of community obligations risks being *weaker* than that available under the default norm of property protection. As a result, rather than more, we risk seeing less compliance with these hierarchical super-norms. Let me explain why this is so.

(a) *Default rules of back-up enforcement for community obligations*

As is the case for other international entitlements, back-up enforcement for community obligations remains essentially limited to (1) reparation and (2) proportional countermeasures. As the ILC Commentary notes, "[t]here has been ... no development of penal consequences for States of breaches of these fundamental norms. For example, the award of punitive damages is not recognized in international law even in relation to serious breaches of obligations arising under peremptory norms."[70] At the same time, when it comes to "serious breach" of *jus cogens* – defined as "gross or systematic failure" to comply with *jus cogens*[71] – states do have an obligation to "cooperate to bring to an end through lawful means" any such breach and not to "recognize as lawful a situation created by a serious breach," or "render aid or assistance in maintaining that situation."[72]

[70] Commentaries to the Draft Articles on the Responsibility of States for Internationally Wrongful Acts (2001), GAOR 56th Session, Supplement no. 10 (A/56/10), at 279.

[71] Article 40.2, ILC Articles.

[72] Article 41, ILC Articles. As noted earlier (*supra*, chapter 3 note 3) the 1996 ILC Draft Articles introduced a distinction between international crimes and international delicts. Although the final 2001 text dropped this distinction, the special consequences attached to international crimes were similar to those set out in Article 41 of the final, 2001 Articles. In addition, however, the 1996 text (Article 52) de-activated some of the excuses otherwise permitted not to offer restitution in kind (including the "burden out of all proportion" justification in what is now Article 35, see *supra* text at chapter 5 note 12) or not to pay compensation (see *supra*, chapter 5 note 12) when it came to

However, other than the UN Security Council acting to maintain international peace and security, and enforcement regimes set up under specific treaties (such as the International Criminal Court, regional human rights treaties and the Kyoto Protocol), there is no collective enforcement or punishment mechanism in international law. Even collective enforcement by the UN Security Council is seriously hampered as it is frequently paralyzed by the veto of one of the five permanent members. Indeed, this is especially the case when the Security Council is faced with *jus cogens* questions such as an alleged genocide or gross human rights violations (witness the reluctance of Russia in the Kosovo crisis or the reluctance of China in the Darfur crisis).[73]

Moreover, it is not just that community obligations are, notwithstanding their higher goal, backed up by more or less the *same* instruments as entitlements protected as property. The situation is worse than that. There is a genuine

international crimes. Interestingly, such de-activation was not maintained in the final text of what is now Article 41.

[73] At the 2005 UN World Summit, the UN General Assembly did, however, make the following commitments: "The international community, through the United Nations . . . has the responsibility to use appropriate diplomatic, humanitarian and other peaceful means, in accordance with Chapters VI and VIII of the Charter, to help to protect populations from genocide, war crimes, ethnic cleansing and crimes against humanity. In this context, we are prepared to take collective action, in a timely and decisive manner, through the Security Council . . . on a case-by-case basis . . . should peaceful means be inadequate and national authorities are manifestly failing to protect their populations from genocide, war crimes, ethnic cleansing and crimes against humanity" (UN General Assembly Resolution, A/Res/60/1 (2005), para. 139).

risk that back-up enforcement for *jus cogens* and collective obligations turns out to be *weaker* than the general rule.

First, given the inalienable nature of *jus cogens* obligations, states responding to breach (including those specifically injured, say, the state victim of crimes against humanity) cannot engage in reciprocal suspension of the obligation concerned, either as a countermeasure[74] or in the form of treaty suspension or termination.[75] Where a victim of WTO breach can impose reciprocal trade sanctions, a victim of crimes against humanity is *not* allowed to reciprocally commit crimes against humanity against the original wrongdoer. Without such threat of reciprocity, the cost of defection obviously decreases. Equally, as collective obligations (say, those related to human rights or global commons) are held collectively by all parties to the treaty, their bilateral, state-to-state suspension would affect not only the wrongdoer but all other parties to the treaty. Because of these third-party effects, the reciprocal suspension of collective obligations is, by default, prohibited.[76] To use Guzman's terminology of the

[74] Article 50 of the ILC Articles, listing obligations that cannot be affected by countermeasures, including obligations for the protection of fundamental human rights and obligations under peremptory norms of general international law.

[75] Article 60.3 of the VCLT, dis-applying treaty suspension or termination in response to material breach in the case of "provisions relating to the protection of the human person contained in treaties of a humanitarian character, in particular to provisions prohibiting any form of reprisals against persons protected by such treaties."

[76] Article 49 of the ILC Articles stresses that countermeasures may only be taken "against a State which is responsible for an internationally wrongful act," not against third parties. Moreover, the bilateral

three Rs of compliance (reciprocity, retaliation and reputation), when it comes to back-up enforcement of community obligations one thus loses the first R of reciprocity. The very classification of an entitlement as either *jus cogens* or a collective obligation brings about a ban on reciprocal suspension of the entitlement.[77]

Second, even though all states (or all states party to the legislative-type treaty) have a right to invoke responsibility for breach of community obligations,[78] the very nature of these obligations often means that no state in particular will actually invoke this right and challenge the wrongdoer. This is because violations of *jus cogens* (say, genocide) or collective obligations (say, those related to global commons such as the ozone layer or the high seas) may not affect any other state in particular. Sometimes they do not materially affect other states at all (as is the case when a government

suspension of collective obligations would also violate the *pacta tertiis* rule (Article 34, VCLT and, for *inter se* suspensions of multilateral treaties, Article 41.1(b)(i), VCLT, discussed *supra* text at note 166).

[77] Moreover, even if reciprocal suspension were permitted, for most violations of *jus cogens* it would not offer much of an incentive to end the violation: few states would feel compelled to stop, for example, genocide because another state threatens to commit genocide on its own population. This problem of back-up enforcement for *jus cogens* stems, however, from the nature of the subject matter itself; not the legal classification of inalienability.

[78] Article 48.1, ILC Articles: "Any State other than an injured State is entitled to invoke the responsibility of another State . . . if: (a) The obligation breached is owed to a group of States including that State, and is established for the protection of a collective interest of the group; or (b) The obligation breached is owed to the international community as a whole."

abuses the human rights of its own population). This creates a collective action problem where more often than not states are unwilling to bear the cost (both economic and political) of enforcing an obligation that does not individually and/or materially affect them. In this sense, the difference between a common or public good and a good that does not belong to anyone (i.e., between the "common heritage of mankind" and *res nullius*) is small. In both cases, no one may effectively protect the good. Note, however, that, unlike the first feature undermining back-up enforcement for community obligations (ban on reciprocal suspension), this second feature is a result of the nature of the subject matter itself, not of the legal classification of inalienability.

Third, even if a state, not specifically affected, were willing to take up the role of policeman in the collective interest, it can only request cessation and reparation.[79] It is generally accepted[80] (with notable exceptions,

[79] Article 48.2 of the ILC Articles, with the limitation that reparation can only be requested "in the interest of the injured State or of the beneficiaries of the obligation breached."

[80] Article 54, ILC Articles: "This chapter does not prejudice the right of any State, entitled under article 48, paragraph 1 to invoke the responsibility of another State, to take *lawful* measures against that State to ensure cessation of the breach and reparation in the interest of the injured State or of the beneficiaries of the obligation breached," (emphasis added). The reference to lawful measures is generally understood as excluding countermeasures which, by definition, are unlawful but excused. In the ILC Commentary to Article 54 (p. 355, para. 6), state practice is reviewed and the following conclusion is made: "the current state of international law on countermeasures taken in the general or collective interest is uncertain. State practice is sparse and involves a limited number of States. At present there appears to be no

however[81]) that under current international law, such a policing nation – unless it is specifically injured (say, itself the victim of aggression) – does *not* have the right to take individual countermeasures. In other words, it cannot resort to the ultimate and most important back-up enforcement instrument available for standard breaches of international

clearly recognized entitlement of States referred to in article 48 to take countermeasures in the collective interest." Similarly, after an exhaustive review of state practice, another author concludes: "a close examination of the cases . . . in which states seemed to be acting in the name of collective interests cannot determinatively lead to the conclusion that there is an established customary or other rule of international law permitting resort to such measures" (Eleni Katselli, "*Countermeasures, the Non-Injured State and the Idea of International Community*," 2005, at 277, DPhil thesis on file with the author). According to Katselli, "states have been hesitant to resort to countermeasures whenever not individually injured because they believed that they had an obligation to refrain from doing so . . . states not only have been reluctant to clearly spell out that they were acting on the basis of a right under international law, but they also stated that doing so would be in violation of international law" (*ibid.*, at 226).

81 See Christian Tams, *Enforcing Obligations* Erga Omnes *in International Law* (Cambridge: Cambridge University Press, 2005), 250 (finding, after an exhaustive survey of state practice, that "it seems justified to conclude that present-day international law recognizes a right of all States, irrespective of individual injury, to take countermeasures in response to large-scale or systematic breaches of obligations *erga omnes*"). More narrowly, the 2005 Resolution on Obligations *Erga Omnes* in International Law of the Institute of International Law provides in Article 5(c): "Should a widely acknowledged grave breach of an *erga omnes* obligation occur, all the States to which the obligation is owed . . . are entitled to take non-forcible counter-measures under conditions analogous to those applying to a State specifically affected by the breach."

law. Knowing that for some violations no single state will be individually injured (as in human rights violations), this, in effect, means that the back-up enforcement of countermeasures is, for certain community obligations, not available *at all.* The reason for this prohibition goes back to the power inequalities between states and the fear of smaller states that the most powerful nations will engage in excessive forms of self-help, in this case even where they are not individually affected.[82] Weaker states must, therefore, balance the benefits of more effective enforcement of community obligations, against the risk that the most powerful nations become the ideological policemen of the world in the guise of individually enforcing obligations in the collective interest. Like the first feature impeding back-up enforcement for community obligations (ban on reciprocal suspension), this third feature (ban on individual countermeasures for states not individually injured) results from the legal classification of an entitlement as inalienable. Consequently, a higher level of protection (inalienability) may actually result in fewer back-up instruments.

82 A similar reluctance to collectively enforce *jus cogens* can be found in the VCLT. Articles 65 and 66 thereof grant jurisdiction to the ICJ to examine disputes on the validity of a treaty on *jus cogens* grounds. Given that all states are harmed by breach of *jus cogens* one would think that all states can invoke this procedure. Yet, the wording of Articles 65 and 66 is such that most commentators conclude that only parties to the treaty in question may invoke its invalidity on the ground that it violates *jus cogens*: Andreas Paulus, "*Jus Cogens* in a Time of Hegemony and Fragmentation – An Attempt at a Re-appraisal" (2005), 74 *Nordic J Int L* 297, at 305, and references in footnote 23.

(b) *An assessment: be careful what you wish for*

As Bruno Simma (now ICJ judge) noted, community obligations in a system without community enforcement are doomed to remain in "the world of the 'ought' rather than that of the 'is'."[83] Even though more states have the right to do something about breach of community obligations, in practice fewer states (if any at all) may actually take the initiative. Moreover, those who are willing to act are deprived of the standard instruments of last resort, namely both (1) reciprocal suspension of the obligation breached and (2) individual countermeasures (unless the state is individually injured by the breach). In this sense, community obligations risk experiencing the worst of both worlds: they lack an effective community-based enforcement mechanism (be it under general international law or specific treaty regimes) and, on top of that, are deprived of the normal back-up of individual enforcement, be it reciprocal suspension or countermeasures.[84]

[83] Bruno Simma, "Does the UN Charter Provide an Adequate Legal Basis for the Individual or Collective Responses to Violations of Obligations *Erga Omnes*?," In Jost Delbruck (ed.), *The Future of International Law Enforcement: New Scenarios – New Law?* (Berlin: Duncker and Humblot, 1993), 125. Or as Ian Brownlie put it more bluntly in respect of *jus cogens*: "the vehicle does not often leave the garage": Ian Brownlie, "Discussion Statement," in Antonio Cassesse and Joseph Weiler (eds.), *Change and Stability in International Law-Making* (Berlin: Walter de Gruyter, 1988), 110.

[84] Philip Allott speaks of a fundamental tension between contemporary international society and contemporary international law: "The tension is between what has been the intrinsically *bilateral* character of

In some respects, and quite paradoxically, the *actual* protection of international entitlements is, therefore, inversely related to how strongly international law *aims* or *pretends* to be protecting the entitlement. This largely explains why we sometimes see less, rather than more, compliance with those norms of international law that are most strongly protected. Perversely, promotion to this higher status may therefore reduce instead of increase actual levels of compliance.[85] As a result, stakeholders in regimes such as trade or environmental protection who are normally anxious to elevate "their" norms to the status of community obligations in an effort to transcend the debasing tit-for-tat horse-trading between states[86] must realize what they are asking for. Taking reciprocity away from a treaty regime without replacing it with a sufficiently solid community may actually weaken rather than strengthen the effectiveness of the treaty. Put differently, it is wrong to presume that promotion to *jus cogens* or collective obligation

international legal accountability and an incipient international *social* responsibility": Philip Allott, *Eunomia: New Order for a New World* (New York: Oxford University Press, 1990), at 333.

85 Promotion to the status of collective or *erga omnes partes* obligation could, thereby, achieve the opposite of what the Institute of International Law has in mind when defining such obligations, namely "in view of their common values *and concern for compliance*": 2005 Resolution on Obligations *Erga Omnes* in International Law, Article 1(b), emphasis added. Rather than more, less compliance could follow.

86 In respect of trade see, for example, Sungjoon Cho, "The WTO's *Gemeinschaft*" (2004), 56 *Alabama LR* 483, and Chios Carmody, "WTO Obligations as Collective" (2006), 17 *EJIL* 419. For the environment, see Michael J. Sandel, "Editorial, It's Immoral To Buy the Right To Pollute," *NY Times*, 15 December 1997, at A23.

automatically leads to better protection and enforcement. On the contrary, quite the opposite may be true.[87]

As discussed in respect of the fall-back rule of property protection, what I called community costs may still create sufficient incentives for states to comply with community obligations. Indeed, one would expect that, for example, reputation costs or the normative pull of the underlying idea or value will be greater when *jus cogens* is violated as opposed to a mere property rule. In addition, the paradox of community obligations without community enforcement has led to growing demands for alternatives away from state-to-state enforcement. Such alternatives could be (1) to match community obligations with a sufficiently robust community enforcement system (the goal, for example, in the Kyoto Protocol[88]); (2) to give direct standing to affected private parties (as, for example, in the European Court of Human Rights); or (3) to enable international proceedings directly against individual criminals (as, for example, in the International Criminal Court). In addition, there is some evidence that (4) domestic courts are increasingly willing to enforce or give direct effect to certain community obligations, especially *jus cogens*, even where for other norms

[87] See Bruno Simma, "International Crimes: Injury and Countermeasures: Comments on Part 2 of the ILC Work on State Responsibility," in Joseph Weiler *et al.* (eds.), *International Crimes of State: A Critical Analysis of the ILC's Draft Article 19 on State Responsibility* (Berlin: Walter de Gruyter, 1989), 283 ("it is a reason for concern that these new conceptions [of community interest] are being grafted upon international law without support through, and any attempt at, adequate institution-building" (at 315)).

[88] See *supra*, this chapter note 68.

they refuse to do so. Such bifurcation between types of international norms can be seen in the recent US Supreme Court opinion in *Sosa v. Alvarez-Machain* (giving effect to some international law under the Alien Tort Statute, but not to other forms[89]), as well as in the courts of the European Union (denying direct effect to WTO rules,[90] but giving direct effect to most other international law, including scrutiny of UN Security Council resolutions under norms of *jus cogens* or fundamental human rights[91]).

89 *Sosa v. Alvarez-Machain*, 542 US 692 (2004) finding that "federal courts should not recognize claims under federal common law for violations of any international law norm with less definite content and acceptance among civilized nations than the 18th-century paradigms familiar when [the Alien Torts Statute] was enacted" in 1789, namely "offenses against ambassadors, violation of safe conduct, and piracy."

90 Piet Eeckhout, *External Relations of the European Union: Legal and Constitutional Foundations* (New York: Oxford University Press, 2004), at 302ff.

91 *Kadi v. Council of the European Union*, 21 September 2005, Case T-315/01 (under appeal).

7

Conclusion

The insights offered in this book are largely good news for international law. Most commentators regard the lack of centralized law-making and enforcement as the core weakness or original sin of the international legal system. In contrast, one of the core conclusions reached in this book is that the starting point of no collective intervention may actually be one of international law's strongest selling points. It turns international law into the prototype "property regime." In such a regime the default rule is that norms are made, and entitlements transferred, by consent, without collective intervention. For those who believe in individual choice and the free exchange of goods and entitlements as the best way to achieve overall welfare, this is good news. One of the biggest fights within states has been to reduce the influence and power of, first, religion and, later, central governments, over the life and choices of individuals. In international affairs, in contrast, the trajectory is quite the opposite: the starting point is freedom, self-determination and the rule that states can only be bound with their consent. From that vantage point, the quest and major difficulty in international law is rather to find centralized mechanisms to deal with collective problems. Whereas within states the challenge has been how to *reduce* collective intervention, at the inter-state level the challenge is how to *increase* collective intervention. In addition, the book has demonstrated that the default rule of freedom and consensual transfers, that is, the property regime of international law, is a regime that is present not only on the books, but also as a law in action. We saw that even without centralized enforcement, the default rule of "mere" compensation or 1:1 retaliation is generally capable of backing up the relatively high level of property protection, not the least thanks to what I referred to as community costs or informal remedies. The property regime of international law does have a harder time to address the problem of free-riders. Yet, carrots and sticks are available to induce states to consent. Such system of ultimate, albeit often tainted, consent may after all be preferable to a centralized law-maker imposing treaties by fiat. The property regime of international law and its general absence of centralized enforcement does make it more difficult, however, (1) to *increase* protection to the level of inalienability (as in *jus cogens* and collective obligations), where more community is needed to ensure appropriate back-up enforcement as well as (2) to *decrease* protection to the level of liability protection (as in unilateral takings of entitlements subject only to compensation), where collective valuation of the value or price of entitlements is a *sine qua non.* Yet, in those areas where international law is most developed and sophisticated, one can expect a growing number of entitlements protected either as inalienable or under a mere liability rule.

In sum, the core message of this book is that optimal protection of international law implies variable protection of international law. Given the expansion and hardening of international law – expansion, to cover fields formerly reserved to domestic law-making; hardening, to include formal enforcement and tribunals with compulsory jurisdiction – international law has reached a degree of maturity that gives it the luxury, indeed the obligation, of variable protection. Gone are the days where international law was largely a derivative of natural law, centered on war and peace and diplomatic relations between sovereign princes. In recent decades, international law has come to address the full panoply of concerns of the regulatory state, ranging from individual human rights to the domestic regulation of commerce and the environment. Faced with similar expansion and diversity, no single domestic legal system requires absolute protection, or imposes the same sanctions, for all legal commitments. Constitutions are normally written in stone, while contracts can simply be renegotiated. Where certain statutory obligations can be bought off, others, such as those under criminal law, cannot be transferred as between private individuals. Theft is sanctioned more heavily than breach of contract, and remedies for constitutional violation are more forceful than those for statutory breach. Far from a concession to weakness, variable protection of international law is the logical result of its success and further refinement. Rather than undermining international law, variable protection takes the normativity of international law seriously and calibrates it to achieve maximum welfare and effectiveness at the lowest cost to contractual freedom and legitimacy.

The specific model developed in this book distinguishes between (1) the allocation of entitlements, (2) the protection of entitlements and (3) back-up enforcement. Within this framework, I have focused on step 2, namely: how strongly international entitlements should be *protected*, and distinguished between inalienability (no *inter se* transfers), property rules (transfers only by mutual consent) and liability rules (unilateral takings are permissible subject to compensation).

The main claim resulting from this analysis is that, by default, international law ought to be protected by a property rule. As in domestic law, to let states transfer their entitlements by mutual consent gives effect to the contractual freedom of states (not to use the word sovereignty). Assuming that states – not international institutions or judges – are best placed to value a state's entitlement, property protection should also maximize inter-state welfare. For those reasons, what I called European absolutism (favoring uniform inalienability) and American voluntarism (favoring uniform liability protection and efficient breach) are undesirable as a fall-back rule. Moreover, as the book demonstrates (in chapter 5), they are also descriptively mistaken as current rules of general international law do, indeed, impose property protection: with limited exceptions, international law entitlements can be altered or transferred *inter se* (they are not inalienable) and their goal is restitution or specific performance, not compensation or efficient breach (as in a liability regime).

Although it may, at first sight, be surprising to see an inherently weak system, such as international law, strongly protect its entitlements as property, this apparent puzzle can be explained: it is largely because of – not despite – the weaknesses of international law that international entitlements are, by default, protected as property. More particularly, it is because of the absence and/or costs of a collective valuation mechanism that a liability rule under current international law is difficult to implement. These weaknesses of international law do not stop, or prevent it, from the relatively high level of property protection. Rather it is those weaknesses that explain the default rule of property protection.

The model developed in this book also shows that any decision on how strongly to *protect* an entitlement (step 2) must take account of the consent-based *allocation* of entitlements (step 1). In particular, inalienability may not be optimal to attract widely diverse states to participate in treaty regimes nor to prevent them from exiting such regimes. The consent-based allocation of entitlements further explains why the standard reason of free-load to shift from property to liability protection does not normally work in international law (treaties cannot be imposed on states without their consent). Finally, the consent-based allocation of entitlements justifies limits on back-up enforcement (weaker back-up enforcement may enable participation and prevent exit) and explains why 1:1 retaliation is the default rule for countermeasures in international law.

Equally, the decision on how strongly to *protect* an entitlement (step 2) must take account of the peculiar *back-up enforcement* of international law (step 3). In particular, the lack of centralized enforcement may militate against both inalienability (which requires strong community enforcement to prevent transfers) and liability protection (which necessitates an effective collective valuation system to assess liability).

At the same time, the book has demonstrated how the generally weak formal instruments of back-up enforcement of international law – compensation and 1:1 retaliation – do not undermine the default rule of property protection, nor the importance of setting variable levels of protection. On the contrary, in addition to the formal remedies of compensation and 1:1 retaliation, what drives compliance is what I have called community costs (such as reputation, fear of emulation, community pressure, the normative pull of ideas and values, and/or an urge to protect a particular institution or the international legal system more generally). And it is exactly the perception of how strongly entitlements are *protected* (under step 2) that triggers and determines the level of those costs (under step 3). Community costs are, in many cases, the "kicker" that back-up property protection in international law. As a result, the default rule of property protection is not only a rule on the books but also the norm of international law in action.

With the default rule of property protection in mind, the model of variable protection developed in this book has also demonstrated that the further refinement and development of international law may increasingly justify inalienability as well as liability rules. In particular, the increasing availability of international courts and tribunals (as in the field of human rights and international criminal law), as well as multilateral oversight (as under the Kyoto Protocol) may justify and enable, respectively, inalienability and liability protection. That said, the current criteria for *jus cogens* and collective obligations – both having inalienable features – would benefit from a more objective analysis. Such analysis should center on externalities, moralisms or incommensurability, and paternalism as grounds for inalienability, rather than what is now an inherently subjective assessment of the values or importance of the norms or treaty concerned.

Similarly, defining collective obligations – from which *inter se* modifications or transfers are prohibited – should not be linked to the importance or value of the treaty. On the contrary, as illustrated in emissions trading under the Kyoto Protocol, property protection (instead of inalienability) can be more effective and can maximize welfare even where it addresses core objectives such as combating global warming. Indeed, when it comes to back-up enforcement, "promoting" a norm to collective obligation status may well reduce, rather than increase, overall levels of compliance, especially when such promotion to community obligation is not matched with a system of community enforcement. Advocates of promoting WTO or certain environmental obligations to the status of community obligations must therefore be careful what they wish for.

An equally careful analysis is required before protecting treaties under a mere liability rule (or take-and-pay principle). The standard reasons to move from property to liability protection in international law are hold-out and high transaction costs. Yet, liability rules should only be considered when a collective valuation mechanism (such as an international tribunal) is available to objectively assess the value of entitlements that states could then unilaterally take from each other. Hence, when what I called American voluntarists and other critics of international law argue for liability rules or a system of efficient breach in the international context, they must be careful what they wish for: a liability regime requires more (not fewer) international institutions and more (not less) central intervention in what is otherwise the free market of entitlements. Moreover, liability rules are more appropriate where entitlements relate to fungible goods (such as investment or trade) rather than unique goods, that is, goods that are more difficult to valuate because of subjective elements. Before installing a liability regime, any gains that can be made in transaction costs or flexibility must also be weighed against the losses of making credible commitment more difficult and potentially exacerbating inequalities between states. Indeed, where the take-and-pay principle works for the rich and powerful but not for the poor or relatively weak it is unlikely to maximize welfare, nor would it be equitable. Finally, and realizing that this objection applies to the broader law and economics approach of this book, treaty negotiators must be aware that since states may not internalize costs nor maximize overall state welfare, liability protection may leave some entities worse off and, therefore, not be Pareto desirable. This risk is particularly grave where entitlements affect non-state actors (as is the case for human rights treaties and, to some extent, WTO obligations). Since states are not unitary actors, even where overall state welfare increases or is left intact, private parties within the state may suffer. As in NAFTA, it may then be necessary to give direct standing to private parties, victim of, for example, expropriation, before moving to a liability scheme.

The purpose of this book was not to offer fixed rules or solutions on how particular norms of international law ought to be protected. Rather, the book offers a baseline (the default rule of property protection) and a matrix of considerations (leading to either inalienability or liability protection) that can guide diplomats, treaty negotiators, judges and other stakeholders when framing and implementing international law. The outcome under this matrix is likely to be different depending on who or which state makes it and will vary across international organizations, treaties and norms. It can even diverge as between norms in the same treaty. Yet, what counts is that law-makers and law-enforcers take the need and appropriateness of varying levels of protection seriously, reach agreement and articulate how and how strongly a particular norm or treaty must be protected and adapt back-up enforcement accordingly. It is these types of refinements that will guarantee the effectiveness and legitimacy of international law and, with it, its long-term survival.

REFERENCES

Aggarwal, Vinod and Cédric Dupont, "Collaboration and Coordination in the Global Political Economy," in John Ravenhill (ed.), *Global Political Economy* (Oxford: Oxford University Press, 2004)

Allott, Philip, *Eunomia: New Order for a New World* (New York: Oxford University Press, 1990)

Axelrod, Robert, *The Evolution of Cooperation* (New York: Basic Books, 1985)

Baron, Jane and Jeffrey Dunoff, "Against Market Rationality: Moral Critiques of Economic Analysis in Legal Theory" (1996), 17 *Cardozo LR* 431

Bebchuk, L. A. and L. Kaplow, "Optimal Sanctions and Differences in Individuals' Likelihood of Avoiding Detection" (1993), 13 *Int Rev L Econ* 217

Becker, Gary, "Crime and Punishment: An Economic Approach" (1968), 76 *J Polit Econ* 169

Bederman, David J., "Counterintuiting Countermeasures" (2002), 96 *AJIL* 817

Been, Vicki and Joel C. Beauvais, "The Global Fifth Amendment? NAFTA's Investment Protections and the Misguided Quest for an International 'Regulatory Takings' Doctrine" (2003), 78 *NYULR* 30

Benvenisti, Eyal, "Exit and Voice in the Age of Globalization" (1999), 98 *Michigan LR* 167

Bianchi, Andrea, "International Law and U.S. Courts: The Myth of Lohengrin Revisited" (2004), 15 *EJIL* 751

Blume, Lawrence and Daniel L. Rubinfeld, "Compensation for Takings: An Economic Analysis" (1984), 72 *California LR* 569

Bolton, John, "Is There Really 'Law' in International Affairs?" (2000), 10 *Trans L Contemp Probs* 1

Boyle, Alan, "Codification of International Environmental Law and the International Law Commission: Injurious Consequences Revisited," in Alan Boyle and David Freestone (eds.), *International Law and Sustainable Development: Past Achievements and Future Challenges* (Oxford: Oxford University Press, 1999)

"The Gabcikovo-Nagymaros Case: New Law in Old Bottles" (1997) 8 *YB Int Env L* 13

Bradford, William, "In the Minds of Men: A Theory of Compliance with the Laws of War" (2004), 36 *Arizona St LJ* 1,243

Bradley, Curtis, "*Breard*, Our Dualist Constitution, and the Internationalist Conception" (1999), 51 *Stanford LR* 529

"International Delegations, the Structural Constitution, and Non-Self-Execution" (2002), 55 *Stanford LR* 1,571

Brimayer, Benjamin, "Bananas, Beef and Compliance in the WTO: The Inability of the WTO Dispute Settlement Process to Achieve Compliance from Superpower Nations" (2001), 10 *Minnesota J Global Trade* 133

Bronckers, Marco and Naboth van den Broek, "Financial Compensation in the WTO" (2005), 8 *JIEL* 101

Brooks, Richard, "The Efficient Performance Hypothesis" (2006), 116 *Yale LJ* 568

Brousseau, Eric, "Did the Common Law Biased [*sic*] the Economics of Contract . . . and May It Change?" (2001), 6 *L Econ Civ L Countries* 79

Brownlie, Ian, "Discussion Statement," in Antonio Cassesse and Joseph Weiler (eds.), *Change and Stability in International Law-Making* (Berlin: Walter de Gruyter, 1988)

Calabresi, Guido and A. Douglas Melamed, "Property Rules, Liability Rules, and Inalienability: One View of the Cathedral" (1972), 85 *Harvard LR* 1,089

Castells, Manuel, *The Rise of the Network Society* (Oxford: Blackwell, 1996)

Charmody, Chios, "WTO Obligations as Collective" (2006), 17 *EJIL* 419

Charney, Jonathan, "Universal International Law" (1993), 87 *AJIL* 529

Charnovitz, Steve, "Rethinking WTO Trade Sanctions" (2001), 94 *AJIL* 792

Chayes, Abram and Antonia Handler Chayes, *The New Sovereignty: Compliance with International Regulatory Agreements* (Cambridge, Mass.: Harvard University Press, 1995)

Cho, Sungjoon, "The Nature of Remedies in International Trade Law" (2004), 65 *U Pittsburgh LR* 763

"The WTO's *Gemeinschaft*" (2004), 56 *Alabama LR* 483

Coase, Ronald, "The Problem of Social Cost" (1960), 3 *JL Econ* 1

Coffee, J. C., "Paradigms Lost: The Blurring of the Criminal and Civil Law Models – and What Can Be Done about It" (1992), 101 *Yale LJ* 1875

Cogan, Jacob, "Noncompliance and the International Rule of Law" (2006), 31 *Yale J Int L* 189

Coleman, Jules and Jody Kraus, "Rethinking the Theory of Legal Rights" (1986), 95 *Yale LJ* 1335

Cook, Benjamin, "Methods in Its Madness: The Endowment Effect in an Analysis of Refugee Burden-Sharing and Proposed Refugee Market" (2004), 19 *Georgetown Immigr LJ* 333

Cooter, Robert, "Prices and Sanctions" (1984), 84 *Columbia LR* 1,523

Craswell, Richard, "Contract Remedies, Renegotiation and the Theory of Efficient Breach" (1987), 61 *Southern California LR* 629

Delahunty, Robert J., "The Battle of Mars and Venus: Why Do American and European Attitudes toward International Law Differ?" (2006), University of Saint Thomas Legal Studies Research Paper No. 06–15, available at SSRN: http://ssrn.com/abstract=899404, last visited 17 September 2007

Dershowitz, Alan M., *Why Terrorism Works* (New Haven: Yale University Press, 2002)

Dinmore, Guy, "US Sees Coalitions of the Willing as Best Ally," *Financial Times*, 5 January 2006

Diver, Colin, "A Theory of Regulatory Enforcement" (1980), 28 *Pub Pol* 257

Downs, George and David Rocke, *Optimal Imperfection: Domestic Uncertainty and Institutions in International Relations* (Princeton: Princeton University Press, 1995)

Dunoff, Jeffrey and Joel Trachtman, "Economic Analysis of International Law" (1999), 24 *Yale J Int L* 1

Dworkin, Ronald, *Taking Rights Seriously* (Cambridge, Mass.: Harvard University Press, 1975)

Eeckhout, Piet, *External Relations of the European Union: Legal and Constitutional Foundations* (New York: Oxford University Press, 2004)

Ellickson, Robert, *Order without Law: How Neighbors Settle Disputes* (Cambridge, Mass.: Harvard University Press, 1991)

Epstein, Paul, "A Clear View of *The Cathedral*: The Dominance of Property Rules" (1996), 106 *Yale LJ* 2,091

Epstein, Richard, *Takings: Private Property and the Power of Eminent Domain* (Cambridge, Mass.: Harvard University Press, 1985)

Fehr, Ernst and Klaus Schmidt, "A Theory of Fairness, Competition and Cooperation" (1999), 114 *QJ Econ* 817

Ferguson, Niall, *Empire* (London: Basic Books, 2004)

Franck, Thomas, *The Power of Legitimacy among Nations* (New York: Oxford University Press, 1990)

Frank, Robert, "If *Homo Economicus* Could Choose His Own Utility Function, Would He Want One With a Conscience?" (1987), 77 *Am Econ R* 593

Fried, Charles, *Contract as Promise: A Theory of Contractual Obligation* (Cambridge, Mass.: Harvard University Press, 1981)

Friedman, Daniel, "The Efficient Breach Fallacy" (1989), 18 *J Leg Stud* 1

Gereffi, Gary and Frederick Mayer, "Making Globalization Work," February 2004 (paper on file with author)

Gneezy, Uri and Aldo Rustichini, "A Fine Is a Price" (2000), 29 *J Leg Stud* 1

Goldsmith, Jack and Eric Posner, *The Limits of International Law* (Oxford: Oxford University Press, 2005)

Goldstein, Judith *et al.*, "Introduction: Legalization and World Politics" (2001), 54 *IO* 385

Goodman, Ryan and Derek Jinks, "How To Influence States: Socialization and International Human Rights Law" (2004) 54 *Duke LJ* 621

Gordley, James, *The Philosophical Origins of Modern Contract Law* (New York: Oxford University Press, 1991)

Greenspan, Alan, *The Age of Turbulence* (New York: Penguin, 2007)

Grotius, H., *De Jure Belli ac Pacis, Libri Tres* ([1647]; Oxford: Oxford University Press, 1925)

Guzman, Andrew, "The Design of International Agreements" (2005), 16 *EJIL* 612

"International Law: A Compliance Based Theory" (2002), 90 *California LR* 1,823

"Reputation and International Law" (2005), 34 *Georgia J Int Comp L* 379

Hamilton, Edith, *The Greek Way* (New York: W. W. Norton, 1993)

Hanqin, Xue, *Transboundary Damage in International Law* (Cambridge: Cambridge University Press, 2003)

Hart, H. L. A., *The Concept of Law* (Oxford: Oxford University Press, 1961)

Hartje, Volkmar J., "Oil Pollution by Tanker Accidents: Liability versus Regulation" (1984), 24 *Nat Res J* 41

Hathawa, Oona, "Do Human Rights Treaties Make a Difference?" (2002) 111 *Yale LJ* 1935

Hatzis, Aristides, "Civil Law and Economic Reasoning: An Unlikely Pair," Working paper dated 6 February 2005, available at http://papers.ssrn.com/sol3/papers.cfm?abstract_id=661661, last visited 17 September 2007

Henkin, Louis, *How Nations Behave: Law and Foreign Policy*, 2nd edn (New York: Columbia University Press, 1979)

Hohfeld, Wesley N., "Some Fundamental Legal Conceptions as Applied in Judicial Reasoning" (1913, 1917), 23 *Yale LJ* 16; 26 *Yale LJ* 710

Holmes, Oliver Wendell, *The Common Law*, ed. Mark D. Howe ([1881] Cambridge, Mass.: Belknap Press, 1963)

Horn, Henrik, Giovanni Maggi and Robert W. Staiger, "The GATT/WTO as an Incomplete Contract," mimeo, 2006 (available at www.econ-law.se/HMS-5April2006.pdf, last visited 17 September 2007)

Hudec, Robert, "Broadening the Scope of Remedies in WTO Dispute Settlement," in Friedl Weiss and Jochem Wiers (eds.), *Improving WTO Dispute Settlement Procedures* (London: Cameron May Publishers, 2000)

Developing Countries in the GATT Legal System (Aldershot: Gower, 1987)

"Transcending the Ostensible: Some Reflections on the Nature of Litigation between Governments" (1987), 72 *Minnesota LR* 211

Hume, David, *A Treatise of Human Nature*, 2nd edn, (ed. L.A. Selby-Bigge [1739–40] Oxford: Oxford University Press, 1978)

Ikenberry, John, "Strategic Reactions to American Preeminence: Great Power Politics in the Age of Unipolarity," National Intelligence Council Conference Report (July 28, 2003), available at www.cia.gov/nic/confreports__stratreact.htm, last visited 17 September 2007

International Labour Office, *Rules of the Game: A Brief Introduction to International Labour Standards* (Geneva: ILO Publications, 2005)

International Law Commission, Commentaries to the Draft Articles on the Responsibility of States for Internationally Wrongful Acts (2001), GAOR 56th Session, Supplement No. 10 (A/56/10)

Jackson, John, "International Law Status of WTO Dispute Settlement Reports: Obligation To Comply or Option To 'Buy Out'?" (2004), 98 *AJIL* 109

The World Trading System: Law and Policy of International Economic Relations, 2nd edn (Cambridge, Mass.: MIT Press, 1997)

Jørgensen, N., "A Reappraisal of Punitive Damages in International Law" (1997), 68 BYIL 247

Kagan, Robert, *Paradise and Power: America and Europe in the New World Order* (New York: A. A. Knopf, 2003)

Katselli, Eleni, "Countermeasures: The Non-Injured State and the Idea of International Community" (2005), D.Phil. thesis from the University of Durham, on file with the author

Kelly, Claire R., "Enmeshment as a Theory of Compliance" (2005), 37 *NYUJ Int L Polit* 303

Keohane, Robert O., *After Hegemony: Cooperation and Discord in the World Political Economy* (Princeton: Princeton University Press, 1984)

"International Relations and International Law: Two Optics" (1997), 38 *Harvard Int LJ* 487

Kiss, Alexandre and Dinah Shelton, *International Environmental Law*, 3rd edn (Cambridge: Transnational Publishers, 2004)

Koh, Harold, "Why Do Nations Obey International Law?" (1997), 106 *Yale LJ* 2599

Kontorovich, Eugene, "The Constitution in Two Dimensions: A Transaction Cost Analysis of Constitutional Remedies" (2005), 91 *Virginia LR* 1,135

Korobkin, R. B. and T. S. Ulen, "Law and Behavioral Science: Removing the Rationality Assumption from Law and Economics" (2000), 88 *California LR* 1051

Kovenock, Dan and Marie Thursby, "GATT, Dispute Settlement and Cooperation" (1992), 4 *Econ Polit* 151

Krauss, Michael, "Property Rules vs. Liability Rules," in B. Bouckaert and G. De Geest (eds.), *Encyclopedia of Law and Economics* (Cheltenham: Edward Elgar, 1999)

Kronman, Anthony T. "Contract Law and the State of Nature" (1985), 1 *JL Econ Org* 5

"Specific Performance" (1978), 45 *U Chicago LR* 351

Landes, W. M., "Optimal Sanctions for Antitrust Violations" (1983), 50 *U Chicago LR* 652

Langille, Brian "Core Labour Rights – The True Story (Reply to Alston)" (2005), 16 *European J Int L* 409

Lawrence, Robert, "Crimes and Punishments? Retaliation under the WTO" (Washington, DC: Peterson Institute, 2003)

Lazareff, Serge, "Assessing Damages – Are Arbitrators Good at It? Should They Be Assisted by Experts? Should They Be Entitled To Decide *ex aequo et bono*? – Some War Stories" (2005), 6 *J World Investment Trade* 17

Levinson, Daryl J., "Making Governments Pay: Markets, Politics and the Allocation of Constitutional Costs" (2000), 67 *Chicago LR* 345

Levitt, Steven and Stephen Dubner, *Freakonomics: A Rogue Economist Explores the Hidden Side of Everything* (New York: William Morrow, 2005)

Macaulay, Stewart, "Non-Contractual Relations in Business" (1963), 28 *Am Soc Rev* 555

Malacrida, Reto, "Towards sounder and fairer WTO retaliation" (2008), 42 *J World Trade* 3

Mavroidis, Petros, "Remedies in the WTO Legal System: Between a Rock and a Hard Place" (2000), 11 *EJIL* 763

Mearsheimer, John, *The Tragedy of Great Power Politics* (New York: W. W. Norton, 2001)

Mitchell, Shannon K., "GATT, Dispute Settlement and Cooperation: A Note" (1997), 9 *Econ Polit* 97

Morgenthau, Hans, *Politics among Nations: The Struggle for Power and Peace* (New York: A. A. Knopf, 1948)

Morris, Madeline, "The Structure of Entitlements" (1993), 78 *Cornell LR* 822

Morrison, Richard, "Efficient Breach of International Agreements" (1994), 23 *Denver J Int L Pol* 183

Movsesian, Mark, "Enforcement of WTO Rulings: An Interest Group Analysis" (2003), 32 *Hofstra LR* 1

Norman, George and Joel P. Trachtman, "The Customary International Law Game" (2005), 99 *AJIL* 541

Nzelibe, Jide, "The Credibility Imperative: The Political Dynamics of Retaliation in the WTO's Dispute Resolution Mechanism" (2005), 6 *Theoretical Inquiries in Law* 215

Palmeter, David, "The WTO Dispute Settlement System in the Next Ten Years," Presentation at Columbia University Conference on *The WTO at 10: Governance, Dispute Settlement and Developing Countries*, 7 April 2006, available at www.sipa.columbia.edu/wto/pdfs/PalmeterWorkingPaper.pdf, last visited 17 September 2007

Palmeter, David and Stanimir Alexandrov, " 'Inducing compliance' with WTO Dispute Settlement," in Daniel Kennedy and James Southwick (eds.), *The Political Economy of International Trade Law: Essays in Honour of Robert Hudec* (Cambridge: Cambridge University Press, 2002)

Parisi, Francesco, "The Genesis of Liability in Ancient Law" (2001), 3 *Am L Econ R* 82

Paulus, Andreas, "*Jus Cogens* in a Time of Hegemony and Fragmentation – An Attempt at a Re-appraisal" (2005), 74 *Nordic J Int L* 297

Pauwelyn, Joost, "Enforcement and Countermeasures in the WTO: Rules Are Rules – Towards a More Collective Approach" (2000), 94 *AJIL* 621

"The Transformation of World Trade" (2005), 104 *Michigan LR* 1

"A Typology of Multilateral Treaty Obligations: Are WTO Obligations Bilateral or Collective in Nature?" (2003), 14 *EJIL* 907

Petersmann, E.-U., *Constitutional Functions and Constitutional Problems of International Economic Law* (Fribourg: Imprim. St-Paul, 1991)

Pildes, Richard H., "Conflicts between American and European Views of Law: The Dark Side of Legalism" (2003), 44 *Vanderbilt J Int L* 145

Posner, Eric, "Economic Analysis of Contract Law after Three Decades: Success or Failure" (2002), University of Chicago Law and Economics, Olin Working Paper No. 146, available at SSRN: http://ssrn.com/abstract=304977, last visited 17 September 2007

Posner, Eric and Alan Sykes, "An Economic Analysis of State and Individual Responsibility under International Law," February 2006, available at http://papers.ssrn.com/sol3/papers.cfm?abstract_id=885197, last visited 17 September 2007

Posner, Richard, "A Theory of Primitive Society, with Special Reference to Law" (1980), 23 *JL Econ* 1

Putnam, Robert D., "Diplomacy and Domestic Politics: The Logic of Two-Level Games" (1988), 42 *IO* 427

Radin, Margaret J., "Market Inalienability" (1987), 100 *Harvard LR* 1849

Raustiala, Kal, "Form and Substance in International Agreements" (2005), 99 *AJIL* 541

"Refining the Limits of International Law" (2005), 34 *Georgia J Int Comp L* 423

Raustiala, Kal and Anne-Marie Slaughter, "International Law, International Relations and Compliance," in Walter Carlsnaes *et al.* (eds.), *Handbook of International Relations* (London: Sage, 2002)

Reichmann, Jerome, "Of Green Tulips and Legal Kudzu: Repackaging Rights in Subpatentable Innovation" (2000), 53 *Vanderbilt LR* 1,743

Restatement (Second) of Contracts (1979)

Rifkin, Jeremy, *The European Dream: How Europe's Vision of the Future is Quietly Eclipsing the American Dream* (New York: J. P. Tarcher/Penguin, 2004)

Rose-Ackerman, Susan, "Inalienability and the Theory of Property Rights" (1985), 85 *Columbia LR* 931

Rosendorff, B. Peter and Helen Milner, "The Optimal Design of International Trade Institutions: Uncertainty and Escape" (2001), 55 *IO* 829

Rubenfeld, Jed, "Unilateralism and Constitutionalism" (2004), 79 *NYULR* 1,971

Ruggie, John, *Constructing the World Polity: Essays on International Institutionalization* (London: Routledge, 1998)

Sagoff, Mark, "Economic Theory and Environmental Law" (1981), 79 *Michigan LR* 1,393

Sandel, Michael J., Editorial, "It's Immoral To Buy the Right To Pollute," *NY Times*, 15 December 1997, at A23

"Sins of Emission," *The Economist*, 5–11 August 2006, 15

Sanger, David, "A Blink from the Bush Administration," *NY Times*, 5 December 2003

Schuck, Peter H., "A Response to the Critics" (1999), 12 *Harvard Hum Rts J* 385

"Refugee Burden-Sharing: A Modest Proposal" (1997), 22 *Yale J Int L* 243

Schwartz, Alan, "The Case for Specific Performance" (1979), 89 *Yale LJ* 271

Schwartz, Alan and Robert Scott, "Contract Theory and the Limits of Contract Law" (2003), 113 *Yale LJ* 541

Schwartz, Warren and Alan Sykes, "The Economic Structure of Renegotiation and Dispute Resolution in the World Trade Organization" (2002), 31 *J Leg Stud* 179

Scott, Robert and Paul Stephan, *The Limits of Leviathan* (Cambridge: Cambridge University Press, 2006)

"Self-Enforcing International Agreements and the Limits of Coercion" (2004), *Wisconsin LR* 551

Shapiro, Martin and Alec Stone Sweet, *On Law, Politics, and Judicialization* (New York: Oxford University Press, 2002)

Shelton, Dinah, "Normative Hierarchy in International Law" (2006), 100 *AJIL* 291

Simma, Bruno, "Does the UN Charter Provide an Adequate Legal Basis for the Individual or Collective Responses to Violations of Obligations *Erga Omnes*?" in Jost Delbruck (ed.), *The Future of International Law Enforcement: New Scenarios – New Law?* (Berlin: Duncker and Humblot, 1993)

"International Crimes: Injury and Countermeasures: Comments on Part 2 of the ILC Work on State Responsibility," in Joseph Weiler *et al.* (eds.), *International Crimes of State: A Critical Analysis of the ILC's Draft Article 19 on State Responsibility* (Berlin: Walter de Gruyter, 1989)

Simmons, Beth, "International Law and State Behavior: Commitment and Compliance in International Monetary Affairs" (2000), 94 *Am Polit Sc R* 819

Slaughter, Anne-Marie, "International Law and International Relations" (2000), 285 *Recueil des Cours* 9

A New World Order (Princeton: Princeton University Press, 2004)

Steger, Debra, "Dispute Settlement under the NAFTA," 2006 manuscript, available with author

Sunstein, Cass, "Incommensurability and Valuation in Law" (1994), 92 *Michigan LR* 779

Swaine, Edward T., "Rational Custom" (2002), 52 *Duke LJ* 599

Sykes, Alan, "The Economics of Public International Law," John M. Olin Law and Economics Working Paper No. 216, July 2004

"The Remedy for Breach of Obligations under the WTO Dispute Settlement Understanding: Damages or Specific Performance?" in Marco Bronckers and Reinhard Quick (eds.), *New Directions in International Economic Law: Essays in Honour of John H. Jackson* (New York: Springer, 2000)

Tams, Christian, *Enforcing Obligations* Erga Omnes *in International Law* (Cambridge: Cambridge University Press, 2005)

Trachtman, Joel P., "Building the WTO Cathedral" (2006), available at http://ssrn.com/abstract=815844, last visited 17 September 2007

Treitel, G. H., *Remedies for Breach of Contract: A Comparative Account* (Oxford: Clarendon, 1988)

Tyler, Tom, *Why People Obey the Law* (Princeton: Princeton University Press, 2006)

United States General Accounting Office, "Report to the Chairman, Committee on Ways and Means, House of Representatives, World Trade Organization: Issues in Dispute Settlement" (August 2000)

United States Trade Representative, Press Release, "State Sovereignty and Trade Agreements: The Facts," 14 April 2005, at www.ustr.gov/assets/Document_Library/Fact_Sheets/2005/asset_upload_ file870_7578.pdf, last visited 17 September 2007

Vagts, Detlev, "The United States and Its Treaties: Observance and Breach" (2001), 95 *AJIL* 313

Van den Bossche, Peter, *The Law and Policy of the WTO* (Cambridge: Cambridge University Press, 2005)

Verdross, Alfred, "Forbidden Treaties in International Law" (1937), 31 *AJIL* 571

"Jus Dispositivum and Jus Cogens in International Law" (1966), 60 *AJIL* 55

Walt, Stephen M., *Taming American Power: The Global Response to U.S. Primacy* (New York: W. W. Norton, 2005)

Weil, Prosper, "Towards Relative Normativity in International Law" (1983), 77 *AJIL* 413

Weiler, Joseph, "The Geology of International Law – Governance, Democracy and Legitimacy" (2004), 64 *ZaöRV* 547

Weiler, Joseph and Iulia Motoc, "Taking Democracy Seriously: The Normative Challenges to the International Legal System," in Stefan Griller (ed.), *International Economic Governance and Non-Economic Concerns* (European Studies Association of Austrian Publications Series 5, 2003)

Weinstein, N. D., "Optimistic Biases about Personal Risks" (1989), 246 *Science* 1,232

Wiener, Jonathan, "Global Environmental Regulation: Instrument Choice in Legal Context" (1999), 108 *Yale LJ* 677

Wils, Wouter, "Optimal Antitrust Fines: Theory and Practice" (2006), 29 *World Comp L Econ R* 183

Wittich, S., "Awe of the Gods and Fear of the Priests: Punitive Damages in the Law of State Responsibility" (1998), 3 *Austrian R Int Eur L* 31

Wolfrum, Rudiger and Nele Matz, *Conflicts in International Environmental Law* (Berlin: Springer, 2003)

WTO Secretariat, World Trade Report (2007)

Young, Ernest, "Institutional Settlement in a Globalizing Judicial System" (2005), 54 *Duke LJ* 1143

Zoller, Elisabeth, *Unilateral Peacetime Remedies: An Analysis of Countermeasures* (Dobbs Ferry: Transnational Publishers, 1984)

Zurn, Michael and Christian Joerges (eds.), *Law and Governance in Postnational Europe: Compliance beyond the Nation-State* (Cambridge: Cambridge University Press, 2005)

Zurn, Michael and Jurgen Neyer, "Conclusions – The Conditions of Compliance," in Michael Zurn and Christian Joerges (eds.), *Law and Governance in Postnational Europe: Compliance beyond the Nation-State* (Cambridge: Cambridge University Press, 2005)

INDEX

In this index, entries in **bold** denote main entries. The following abbreviations are used.

ABM	Anti-Ballistic Missile Treaty
BITs	Bilateral Investment Treaties
CAC	Convention against Corruption
CBD	Convention on Biological Diversity
CDM	Clean Development Mechanism
DSU	Understanding on Rules and Procedures Governing the Settlement of Disputes
EC	European Communities
ECHR	European Convention of Human Rights
ECtHR	European Court of Human Rights
EU	European Union
FAO	Food and Agriculture Organization
FATF	Financial Action Task Force
GATS	General Agreement on Trade and Services
GATT	General Agreement on Tariffs and Trade
ICC	International Criminal Court
ICJ	International Court of Justice
ILC	International Law Commission
ILO	International Labour Organization
INF	Intermediate-Range Nuclear Forces Treaty
MFN	Most Favoured Nation
NAFTA	North American Free Trade Agreement
OECD	Organization for Economic Cooperation and Development
PCLNE	Paris Convention on Third Party Liability in the Field of Nuclear Energy
SALT	Strategic Arms Limitation Talks

INDEX

TRIPS	Agreement on Trade Related Aspects of Intellectual Property Rights
UN	United Nations
UNCLOS	United Nations Convention of the Law of the Sea
UNESCO	United Nations Educational, Scientific and Cultural Organization
US	United States of America
VCLND	Vienna Convention on Civil Liability for Nuclear Damage
VCLT	Vienna Convention on the Law of Treaties
WTO	World Trade Organization